# Understanding Whiteness
## Unraveling Racism
### Tools for the Journey

Judy Helfand
Laurie Lippin, Ph.D.

Editor: Mark Clippinger
Production Manager: Staci Powers
Production Coordinator: Mary Snelling
Marketing Coordinator: Sara L. Hinckley

Printed in the United States of America

**Thomson Learning Custom Publishing**
**5191 Natorp Blvd.**
**Mason, Ohio 45040**
**USA**

For information about our products, contact us:
**1-800-355-9983**
http://www.custom.thomsonlearning.com

**International Headquarters**
Thomson Learning
International Division
290 Harbor Drive, 2nd Floor
Stamford, CT 06902-7477
USA

**UK/Europe/Middle East/South Africa**
Thomson Learning
Berkshire House
168-173 High Holborn
London WCIV 7AA

**Asia**
Thomson Learning
60 Albert Street, #15-01
Albert Complex
Singapore 189969

**Canada**
Nelson Thomson Learning
1120 Birchmount Road
Toronto, Ontario MIK 5G4
Canada
United Kingdom

Visit us at www.e-riginality.com and learn more about this book and other titles published by Thomson Learning Custom Publishing

ISBN 0-759-31422-5

The Adaptable Courseware Program consists of products and additions to existing Custom Publishing products that are produced from camera-ready copy. Peer review, class testing, and accuracy are primarily the responsibility of the author(s).

# INTRODUCTION

## Welcome

"Understanding Whiteness/Unraveling Racism," is a new kind of diversity course, examining what it means to be white instead of examining only the position, history, and experiences of people of color. The goal is not to place blame, but to better understand the role of white people in the circumstances that surround privilege and oppression.

In our experience the work of understanding whiteness in a white-dominant culture cannot be done in isolation from our lives. It works more effectively for us to have our learning experiences and then return to our communities with new awareness. Often we suggest an assignment of something to do, to see, to try. Then suggest you come together with others to talk about the reality of integrating your new understanding into your life. Understanding whiteness requires dealing with our minds, our thoughts, our feelings, and our behavior.

Participating in understanding whiteness and unraveling racism is a journey—an arduous, difficult journey with many obstacles, especially for white people. There is no cheering from the sidelines, often the opposite. Seldom is anyone going to pat you on the back for doing it. Your friends and family may question you or be threatened by what you are saying or doing. Why do it then? We must stop participating in the perpetuation of an inequitable system that is destroying this country, wounding the next generation of leaders, taking the heart out of many of us, and affecting our very souls. The advantages to the country, and to us as individuals, are enormous. On an organizational level, the future success of businesses and community groups will be greatly affected by their ability to embrace a diverse workforce or membership. On a personal level, only you can answer.

For the record, no one of us alone can unravel racism since racism is systemic and institutionalized in the U.S. and in other countries. It is embedded in the systems that make up our society, for example, the educational system, the economic system, and the political system. One need only look at the resources made available to neighborhoods in which poor people and people of color live to see systemic racism in action. Also, classism is so deeply entrenched with racism that it is difficult to separate the two.

We begin together but you can continue this work in other ways. Hopefully the learnings, insights, actions garnered here will stay with you. Hopefully, you will share what you learn so that others may benefit from your journey. Although we authored this book, we take the journey with you as we continue to do our own work in this area. We are not finished and recognize that we still continue to make mistakes every day as we struggle to change life-long patterns of learned privileged behavior that disadvantages others.

Judy Helfand and Laurie Lippin
Sonoma County 2001

## About the Workbook

This workbook is divided into six sections. Each section has an overview, readings, exercises, and questions for you to consider and write about. Many of the exercises are group or partner activities designed for you to participate in with others. However, if you are taking this course on your own, you can always adapt them to suit your circumstances.

We invite you to personalize this book through journaling. Record your own reactions, reflections, confusions, and insights. You may want to begin right now by jotting down your thoughts on the following questions.

*Reflections on why you're here*

What do I bring to this work?

_____

_____

_____

_____

_____

_____

_____

What do I hope to gain?

_____

_____

_____

_____

_____

_____

## Guidelines for Participation

These guidelines are intended for those of you who are participating in classroom or group discussions. Talking about race is a scary and sensitive subject. Add in the expectation of personal introspection, sharing, and risk taking, and it's clear that you need a safe space for your meetings. Use these guidelines to help in your group conversations:

- Keep all personal information and opinion you hear as confidential. This means that you do not talk about what another person says outside the meeting space.

- Use "I statements." Talk from your own experience and be sure to mark your opinions as your own by saying "As I see it" or "In my experience."

- Share air time with others. Some of us speak out quickly and confidently in groups. Others need more time to gather their thoughts. Try to pay attention so that you don't speak again until everyone else has had a chance. Silence for a few moments or even longer is OK.

- Constructive feedback is welcome. If you react strongly to what someone says, remember we are looking for honesty, which may not be pretty. Judgement or ridicule never aids in uncovering the truth.

- Don't bring up private issues with another person outside the meeting space without permission. For example, ask "I was interested in your growing up story. Is it OK to talk about it more?"

INTRODUCTION

# Section I
## *WHITENESS*

## What Is Whiteness?

Those of us who check "white" on the race/ethnicity category probably don't think much about what "white" means. Most white people aren't aware of their "whiteness" unless they are consciously thinking about diversity. Even then, white is often the background against which people of color stand out as other. Asked to define "white," white folks may stumble, "Well, it's, you know — *white!*" Yet for those who fit into that category, it shapes their lives and their self-image in the world.

Whiteness is an historical, cultural, social, and political category. Our work in understanding whiteness includes beginning to fill out the words in the previous sentence —

- When in American history did "white" become a term used to describe a group of people? How did families identifying as German, Finnish, or Italian, for example, change to identifying as white or simply American?

- Are there any white cultural practices? Is there a white culture? Why do we find it difficult to answer those questions if we are white?

- How have white people been shaped by their social environment? How has racism affected their daily lives?

- How has whiteness been used politically? What current issues center around whiteness?

We're certainly not going to answer all those questions right now. But reading through them alerts you to the work ahead. Throughout the course, after completing some readings or participating in a group exercise, you may want to return to these questions and use them to think about what you've just experienced.

Because whiteness is so often invisible to white people, but not invisible to people of color, the exercises and readings for this section of the workshop are chosen to bring whiteness into focus, helping those of you who are white begin to take responsibility for your identity. You will explore social geography — the racial and ethnic makeup of the neighborhoods you grew up in and your interactions with people both like and unlike you. In another exercise you will ask the question, "When are you white?" The readings for this section also explore the question "What is whiteness?"

Before reading any further, take a few minutes and reflect on where you grew up. Think about daily interactions and relationships in terms of race and ethnicity. Think about the racial boundaries in your community. What did you learn from your family about people who looked different from yourselves? Jot down your thoughts on these questions below. As you explore these questions further during the exercises and discussions, return here to record any new memories or insights.

*Notes on growing up with race and ethnicity*

_____

_____

_____

_____

_____

_____

_____

_____

_____

_____

_____

_____

_____

_____

_____

_____

## Readings: Thinking About Race

The essays and excerpts from books gathered in this section present various viewpoints on race. What all these pieces have in common is that they are written by a person of color and give us an opportunity to see whiteness through non-white eyes.

- In an excerpt from "The Funeral Banquet" Lisa See, a mixed-race woman who looks white and is "Chinese in my heart," talks about living in two worlds—the white world and the Chinese world.

- Lori Tsang describes the elusive reality of race in an excerpt from "Postcards From 'Home."

- "Stop the Lies," by Luis. J. Rodriguez, lists a number of lies about race, most of which are so integrated into our culture that we never think about them.

- "When are you white?" asks Lisa Funderburg in interviewing friends and acquaintances. The responses are varied and revealing.

- Finally, we've included an essay by James Baldwin, "On Being White and Other Lies," that describes what immigrants gave up to become white in the U.S.

## The Funeral Banquet (excerpt)

*As a woman whose racial and ethnic heritage is not evident in her face, Lisa See has some insightful thoughts on how thoroughly appearance influences ones treatment. The following is excerpted from "The Funeral Banquet," copyright (c) 1998 by Lisa See. From* HALF AND HALF *by Claudine Chiawei O'Hearn, copyright (c) 1998 by Claudine Chiawei O'Hearn. Used by permission of Pantheon Books, a division of Random House, Inc.*

In the prologue for *On Gold Mountain*, I wrote that I didn't look Chinese but I was Chinese in my heart. When I wrote those words, I worried that I was being presumptuous and that the Chinese community would not take kindly to it. As in, "How dare you claim to be a Chinese when you don't look the part?" That didn't happen, because I didn't embarrass anyone. As one of my cousins once said, "If you do something or say something that is bad, it reflects on the entire family." That idea ripples out across all of Chinese culture. If you do something bad or embarrassing, it not only reflects on the family but on the entire race. (As an aside, think about the pressure that puts on Asian American writers as they sit down at their computers to write an article or book. Think about how that idea affects every career or life choice an Asian American makes.)

Still, I have had these bizarre moments when a couple of Chinese discuss my appearance in front of me as though I weren't there. "Her face is long. You know, some Cantonese look like that." Or, "She's slim, not fat like the usual American." "Look at her eyes. I had an uncle with eyes like that." "But her hair. . ." This last always brings the conversation to a disquieting close.

What I hadn't anticipated was that my statement about being Chinese in my heart would make Caucasians batty. "What do you mean you feel Chinese in your heart? You don't look Chinese!" Even more than their comments, I've been surprised and interested by the flashes of bewilderment—and sometimes disgust—on their faces. I think it comes down to this: Why would anyone choose to be other than white? Why would anyone forsake the inherent privilege that being white allows us in this country?

The other related question I've gotten these last couple of years is "Have you ever felt discriminated against?" Of course not. I have red hair, freckles. In this country, people look at a face and when they see white, they make a whole range of decisions based on the assumption that what they're seeing is true. I look white, therefore I am white. How easy it must be for me to say I'm Chinese in my heart when I haven't had to pay the price. No one's ever turned me down to rent an apartment based on the color of my skin. No one has ever called me a slant-eye, a gook, a Chinaman. No one has ever accused me of being good at math or computers or science because of my racial background.

Nevertheless, I have paid a price. If in the white world I'm white, in the Chinese world I'm white, too. I've had relatives—100 percent Chinese-blood relatives—say to me, "Oh! so-and-so is Caucasian just like you." I've had waiters in Chinese restaurants tell me I shouldn't order a particular dish because it's not for Caucasian tastes, or, even more insulting, put a fork by my plate. Those people look at me and, just like their Caucasian counterparts, see only my white face with these freckles. What I want to say to them is, "My great-grandfather worked on the railroad, goddamn it! I know how I'm related to every single one of my relatives. My family suffered from the old laws barring marriage between Chinese and Caucasians, barring the ownership of property (making us land poor but 'stuff' rich), barring the immigration of our other relatives long before you or your family ever thought about America." These are not charitable thoughts, but I have them just the same.

Things have changed since my great-grandparents, grandparents, and even my own parents got married. Mixed marriages and biracial children are now extremely common. I've seen it in the faces of people who come to hear me speak in bookstores in Minneapolis, Denver, Seattle. I've seen it in the world faces of the nurses at Good Samaritan Hospital. I've seen it in the faces of the kids my children play with. Those kids may look one way, but how can I or anyone else tell whose side of the family they'll take after when the mother might be from Baltimore, Bombay, or Beijing and the father from Bozcaada, Budapest, or Bogotá? In the 1990s, I'm still an aberration, but in another ten, twenty, thirty years, Americans will look at each other and—just like they do with me now—really not know who someone is by their face. When I say that in lectures, there's a moment when I see smiles on faces and people nodding agreeably. Very quickly, that turns to a collective look of confusion as people play this out in their minds. What would it be like to shake someone's hand and not know what they are?

### Postcards from "Home" (excerpt)

*In "Postcards from 'Home'," Lori Tsang talks about her confusion with her identity that stemmed from having parents brought up in different cultures— a Chinese father who spent his childhood in China before coming to the United States and a Chinese- Jamaican mother. In this excerpt, she discusses both culture and race. "Postcards from 'Home'" copyright (c) 1998 by Lori Tsang. From* HALF AND HALF *by Claudine Chiawei O'Hearn, copyright (c) 1998 by Claudine Chiawei O'Hearn. Used by permission of Pantheon Books, a division of Random House, Inc.*

My friend Ethelbert asks me if I have any African heritage. He's editing an anthology of African American poetry, and he's trying to include me. It seems all my friends are going to be in this anthology, and I want to be, too. "You mean, genealogically?" I ask, and he says yes. I think about saying that, according to Ivan Van Sertima, the human race started in Africa, so everybody is African. But what comes out of my mouth is "Well, not that I know of."

But I first learned how to be "Asian American" from African Americans. After we moved to Indiana, we lived in another white neighborhood. The only black person in our neighborhood was this real light-skinned kid who was adopted by a Jewish couple who didn't know he was black when they adopted him. They didn't even tell him he was black until he was already pretty grown. The junior high school I went to was the only naturally integrated junior high school in northern Indianapolis. Not because of this one kid, but because there was a black neighborhood in that district. I used to ride my bike over there to see my friends Sherril and Elaine. There were no other Chinese, or even Asians, in our neighborhood. I remember another Chinese girl telling me that when her parents first moved to Indianapolis, they looked through the names in the phone book so they could find other Chinese. And in the summer, our whole family used to go to a special camp where Chinese families in the Midwest got together to be with other Chinese.

But race, like sex, was something my parents never discussed—as if it were something shameful. When two non-white Americans meet, each of us understands that we share the common experience of racial prejudice; it's our individual reactions to that experience that may be different: anger, self- pity, denial. Confusion. Probably, my parents didn't talk much about race because they didn't understand it. After all, who really does? The complex web of relationships among race, culture, and skin color remains just as elusive a reality as the relationships among sex, power, and love. Like water, it takes the shape of whatever contains it—whatever culture, social structure, political system. But like water, it slips through your fingers when you try to hold it. And maybe it was this, the unspoken, which remained elusive yet suspended in the silences, that drew me closer to my African American friends—the experience of being different from the majority of white people, the experience of racial prejudice.

### Stop the Lies

*"Stop the Lies" by Luis J. Rodriguez was included in a special issue on whiteness of* The Hungry Mind Review: The National Book Magazine, *Issue 45, Spring 1998. Luis J. Rodriguez is an award-winning poet, essayist, journalist and children's book writer. His most recent works include a children's book,* America Is Her Name, *and a collection of poetry,* Trochemoche, *both from Curbstone Press. From Luis J. Rodriguez; "Stop the Lies,"* The Ruminator Review, *Spring 1998, Issue 45. Copyright (c) 1998 The Ruminator Review. Reprinted with permission of The Ruminator Review.*

In 1997 President Bill Clinton dared to open up the race debate with a number of so-called town hall meetings. In my view, many of these meetings were farcical and insulting. The basic lies were not challenged. I believe because of this the lies were thus perpetuated. Apologies and meaningless gestures of retribution are even more insulting. They only give the lies more adherence in our conscience.

You want to talk about race in America? Then stop the lies.

Stop the lie that Aryans were white and superior. According to J. M. Roberts in *A Short History of the World* (Oxford University Press, 1993), they were central Asian warriors and nomads who settled into India, Iran (which means "Land of the Aryans"), and eastern Europe some 2,000 years before Christ. And although they contributed much (including the horse-drawn chariot, the Indo-European family of languages, and the Vedas), they also held back certain aspects of culture and development in the areas they conquered.

"The Aryans had no culture so advanced as what they found," says Roberts. "Writing disappears with their arrival, not emerging again until the middle of the first millennium B.C.; cities, too, had to be reinvented, and when they appear again lack the elaboration and order of their Indus Valley predecessors."

Stop the lie that Jesus Christ was white. He was an Aramaic-speaking brown man who never set foot in Europe. The first Christians were from the Semitic regions of the Mediterranean, including Northern Africa, where many of the original Christians, including the Coptic Church of Egypt and Ethiopia, still exist. The teachings of Jesus Christ are no less profound. He doesn't have to be white!

Stop the lie that Europe civilized the world. A case can be made that it was the other way around. For example, the shaping forces of the European renaissance of the fourteenth to seventeenth centuries include the opening of trade with China, the Moors' 800 year rule of Spain, the first circumnavigation of the world by Ferdinand Magellan, the conquest of the Americas (including the looting of gold and silver that fueled the engines of Europe's incipient capitalist economy), and the slave trade in Africa. Gypsies, Huns, Arabs, Tartars, Jews, and others have all contributed to "civilization" in Europe.

Stop the lie that humans can be delineated by race. There are no anthropological, spiritual, or biological grounds for such a concept. The American notion of race is a relatively recent construct predicated on the oppression and exploitation of one people over others.

"The traffic grew with the profits—the shuttle service importing human chattel to America in overcrowded ships," writes Earl Conrad in his 1967 book *The Invention of the Negro* (Paul S. Eriksson Publishers). "It was on these ships that we find the beginnings—the first crystallizations--of the curious doctrine which was to be called 'white supremacy.'. . . Among the first men to develop attitudes of supremacy were the slaveship crew."

This doctrine was later supported by pseudo-scientific papers that declared Africans, Amerindians, and Asians as inferior to Europeans, including from the mighty pens of such scholars as Kant and freedom defenders as Thomas Jefferson! According to Emmanuel Chukwudi Eze in *Race and the Enlightenment* (Blackwell Press, 1997), Kant stated in his master work, *Physical Geography,* that humanity is at its greatest perfection in the race of the whites." And Jefferson had this to say in "Laws," from *Notes on the State of Virginia*: "Unfortunate difference of color, and perhaps of faculty is a powerful obstacle to the emancipation of [black] people."

Stop the lie that we live in a monolithic culture. What we call America was forged with the ideas, blood, sweat, labor, laws, and cultural contributions of the indigenous peoples of the land as well as Africans, Eastern Europeans, Italians, Spanish, French, British, Irish, Chinese, Japanese, mixed-bloods-and on and on. Things we take for granted, such as cowboys, jazz, karate, chocolate, corn, tobacco, paper, surfing, gunpowder, pasta, rock-n-roll, and our system of government, have roots in non-European cultures.

Once a white acquaintance came with me to catch a Quebradita dance in Chicago of mostly Mexican and Chicano youth. The young people sported cowboy hats, and leather belts and boots. He looked at me and said, "These kids have no originality—they are trying to be American cowboys!"

You can imagine my response, since those cowboy hats and leather styles originated with the Mexican vaquero (a combination of Moorish-Spanish and Mexican-U.S. Indian influences) and was later appropriated by Americans conquering the West. In fact, the first cowboys were Indians recruited by the Spanish landowners of California and the Southwest!

We also don't properly acknowledge how Native Americans influenced our system of government. In *Indian Givers: How the Indians of the Americas Transformed the World* (Fawcett Columbine Books, 1988), Jack Weatherford credits the Iroquois Confederacy with providing many of the ideas American revolutionists used to frame a new government. "The Americans followed the model of the Iroquois League not only in broad outline but also in many of the specific provisions," writes Weatherford.

James W. Loewen, author of *Lies My Teacher Told Me* (The New Press, 1995), points out that the symbol of the United States, the eagle clutching a bundle of arrows, were symbols of the Iroquois League.

The problem is you can't get rid of racism just by attacking racism. Its strongest foundation as an ideology and practice has been a growing industrial economy. In such growth, industry maintains a brutal competition between the most exploitable workers for the least possible pay. Color privilege is key to this competition.

However, this foundation is eroding. We are entering an era characterized by the "end of work." The technological advances in production, downsizing, and globalization are changing racial politics as we know it. As the nature of work changes—there is simply no longer a need in this country for a large, unskilled, and labor-intensive workforce—so do the concepts, ideologies, and divisions that arose under the previous circumstances.

I have been to the coal country of the Appalachias, the rust belt of the Great Lakes region, and in towns along rural acres of untended farmland, where unemployment has reached over fifty percent, youth are on the corners with nothing to do, and rates of alcoholism, homicide, gang violence, and broken families are at epidemic levels among whites!

The real social division governing how we live and think is that of class. Today class interests are forcing us to look deeper at any so-called unity based on race. But how often have we been told that class issues do not really exist in America?

Stop the lies. Stop the lies. Stop the lies.

Then let's talk.

### When Are You White? (excerpt)

*Taken by the new interest in white studies, Lisa Funderburg decided to bring the issue to the streets, asking "When Are You White?" Funderburg interviews both whites and people of color. We've reprinted some of those interviews.* From Lisa Funderberg, "When Are You White?," *The Ruminator Review,* Spring 1998, Issue 45. Copyright (c) 1998 The Ruminator Review. Reprinted with permission of The Ruminator Review.

I don't want to dis academia, but whiteness studies? Since when is the Commentary a more pertinent text than The Life We Experience? I decided to take this question of whiteness to the streets, so to speak, and conduct my own field study with some fellow Americans. When, exactly, does whiteness show up in our lives? Is it a color, a consciousness, a culture? Is it transitional, transitive, transitory? Immutable? Is it something? Is it nothing? I came up with one question: When are you white? I tried a couple of dry runs, with friends, over the phone. The first, a white woman who lives in a predominantly white New Jersey suburb, said she's most aware of feeling white at PTA meetings, where brown faces are few and far between. Another friend, also a woman and also white, said she feels white when she goes to a large Manhattan hospital for cancer treatment, which currently works out to just about every other day of her life. "I feel so oppressed there," she said, "that to compensate, I become haughty and much more fearless and aggressive than I actually feel, because to behave in any other way is to become an instant minority, which is to be treated without justice or decency. I develop a certain bravado that I don't actually have. And that's white. I think so. I think a lot of white people approach things with a certain sense of entitlement that I don't normally feel." And why does going to the hospital confer minority status? "Because you don't have any control," she explained, "because you have a handful of middle-aged men touching you and telling you what to do and what not to do and you wait for hours on various lines so that somebody can invade your body."

I was ready to collect data, but first, in a Jekyllian moment, I asked myself the question. My answer, at that moment, was that I am almost always white to other people when they hear my voice or learn my name. When they actually meet me, they still assume I'm white because my melanin-challenged features fit their expectations of what white is. The exception is when I'm with the black side of my family, many of whom I strongly resemble, but for pigment. Sometimes, not often, I forget how white I look. I'll be at an all-black party or conference and suddenly I'll glimpse a white face in a mirror, surprised to find that it is my own reflection. But what other people see in me is simply a measure of their myopia. I see identity as more than just what's ascribed, and when I look inward, what I see and feel is other than white. I realized that in order not to lead my subjects, I had to be careful, in asking my question, to avoid putting particular emphasis on either the "when" or the "you."

The strict research protocol to which I adhered lead me first to my own kitchen, where Don Kennedy, a carpenter, was replacing baseboard trim. As happens with even the cheapest of renovations, Don had been in and around my house longer than either of us could have hoped or desired, and so we had become pals. Trading on this new friendship, I stuck a microphone in his face. He was the first of many I spoke to—neighbors, acquaintances, and strangers, some famous, some not, all willing to take on a question that is somewhere between uncomfortable, unexpected, and unanswerable.

Don Kennedy Age: 33
Location: Wyndinoor, Pennsylvania
Occupation: Lead Carpenter
Race/Culture/Ethnicity: White, Irish American

Uh. Hm. When do I think of myself as white? Never. What's color? Okay, I'm trying to think of an answer. I think of myself as white when political issues come up, I guess. But not in general, as a being. When they talk about, I mean, there's such an uprising of, like, Afro-American, know what I mean? I mean, somebody could've been born here three hundred years ago, but they still consider themselves African American. My grandfather doesn't say he's Irish: He says, "I'm American; I was born here." So I kind of have that mind-set of well, fine, but you're not African, really. And when issues come up about affirmative action and jobs, you know? Last week there was something in the paper. Some company was selling products the black community didn't want them to sell because only the black people should get the proceeds from whatever this stuff was, which is kind of crazy, you know what I mean? It's like, You can't do this because you're not black, but he can because he is. I think of myself as white then because what if I was the person selling whatever it was?

Claudia Raab
Age: 47
Location: Philadelphia, Pennsylvania
Occupation: Cooking student, community-builder
Race/Culture/Ethnicity: White, Jewish

When I go in a very black neighborhood I feel very white. When I'm scared by young black men in groups. When I do things that I feel like I'm privileged to do, like buy new cars and houses. That's when I feel white the most, probably, is when I feel privileged.

Aracely Rosales Age: 40
Location: Philadelphia, Pennsylvania
Occupation: Director of Health Education Program
Race/Culture/Ethnicity: Guatemalan American

What do you mean? White as in color, as in skin? When am I white? When I need to be white. I think I have observed and assimilated lots of the culture so that I can actually be like white people in a way that, culturally, I need to be. When I feel like I need to be just like the rest of the people so that I am not pushed aside. When I need to claim a sort of a status or place, you can call it that way, I need to be white.

I wouldn't say you can act it. You just have to be. And I have learned how people are in certain occasions and I know I have to be the same way. Most of the time, it happens in job situations. There, I need to be like the rest of the people that I am with and I need to speak at the same level if it is job-related. Whatever people are talking about, I need to be documented and talk about the same thing. And for me, that's being white, because I'm totally different than what I really am at home, where I don't talk about certain issues and I don't discuss certain situations. For me, culturally speaking, I'm a Latina person, so I wouldn't say I totally forget who I am, and I am not trying to be somebody that I am not. I just need to be like the others.

Let me give you a situation. At the airport. Here I am, just coming from a trip to Guatemala. I'm a different color skin. I definitely have an accent. Anybody can see that I am not a white person. However,

I'm a USA citizen and I have the same rights a white American person has. And I need to show that because otherwise people will discriminate against me immediately, at the first moment they see me. They look at me and the first thing I can sense is, "This person doesn't speak English." So the first thing I do is speak English, to show them I do and I can hear what they're saying and they can talk to me freely. At that very moment there, I'm saying something. The attitude changes. However, still there is a barrier. I'm still a Latina person with a different skin color and eyes and definitely an accent, so they are trying to expect something else from me.

So we are coming inside [customs] and there are two lanes. So the lady, of course a white lady, she says, "Non-residents and residents this way please." I don't pay attention because I know my way. I read. They don't need to tell me. I have already oriented myself and I know where I'm going. So she talks to me again and she says, "Excuse me, this is a USA citizens' lane." I turn to her and say, "I know what I'm doing. I know it's a USA citizens' lane. I can read."

So there, I'm showing her. I need, first of all, to be assertive, which to me means being white. Lots of people—not everybody—but lots of people make assumptions just because of the way you look or the way your accent is.

Jeff Yang
Age: 29
Location: New York, New York
Occupation: Writer and editor of *A. Magazine: Inside Asian America*
Race/Culture/Ethnicity: Asian, second-generation Chinese American

I would actually have to say never. I think that whatever whiteness, like a residue, has clung to me from my years of exposure and culture and training, it never goes beyond the skin. It never even sinks into the pores. And I'm at a point now, in fact, where the more I'm with white people, the less white I feel. You'd think that there was a stage in which you would be assimilated in the Star Trek "Borg" sense, not the racial sense. That you would become part of this larger fleshly being, this body of society that, in its default, is white. Because, after all, whiteness isn't actually something somebody is. It's something somebody ends up being when they're not anything else in our society. You don't say, "That's my white friend." But if the person's anything other than just plain old vanilla, you have to say, "Oh yeah, this is my black friend, this is my Asian friend." White culture is the option we rest on; it's the way we go when no choice is made. When I talk on the phone with you, when I don't evince any kind of accent, you assume I'm white until I tell you my last name or until I meet you. And that's happened to me any number of times.

I may have been at my most white when I was back in school, before I was sensitive to being anything different. It's funny. Back then is when I had my most prominent incidences of casual racism, the kind that kids deal with: people laughing at you, calling you Ching Chong names, making Chop Sake gestures, comparing you on a good day to Bruce Lee. But back then, it didn't make sense as a race thing. It was just another form of difference that I bore up with and that set me apart. No different from being short, let's say, or fat, or nearsighted or any of the other things many other kids in my school were.

That was the beginnings of gawky adolescence, when people become aware enough of difference to point it out and are still so unaware of diplomacy as to do so in public. And so back then, I still felt, for what it's worth, White with a capital W, even though I knew my skin was different and my eyes were different and my hair was different, or my culture, my food, and my parents were different. It wasn't until I was older—once people were sensitive enough to no longer display that casual or arrogant differentiation of race—that I started to pick up on those subtle things which in some ways forever separate nonwhite from white.

I went to school at Harvard, which has a certain set of traditions and a certain inbred heritage, and here are some things you notice: When non-whites sit together at a table, they're called isolationists. It's pointed out: "How come you always sit with black people? How come you always sit with Asian people?" When white people sit together, they're friends. I'd go into restaurants with a group of friends, most of whom were white, and just happen to be left out of the party by the maitre d'. He'd say, "Will it be five?" "No, it'll be six, because we have our Asian friend."

These aren't things to be angry about, or even things to necessarily allow to abrade your skin. They're things that are realities when whiteness is the default, like in our society.

When I go to places like Hawaii or California, places where white as default does not exist—where, in some cases even, Asian as default exists—it's a different world and a different feeling. And makes me understand, briefly, what it means not to be white but to be in a white man's world, you know, with the hand of the majority. You asked when am I white. If I'm in that sentence, if it's about me, the answer is never. When am I white to you? I could be right now. I could be anytime that there isn't that telltale evidence that I'm not. Your question presupposes the idea that whiteness or blackness or any kind of race-ness, to horribly mangle that idea, is transitional. It's something that you can endow, something you can move through, something you can remove at times.

### On Being White and Other Lies

*"On Being White and Other Lies," by James Baldwin (1924-1987), was first pub-*
*lished in the popular African-American magazine* Essence *in 1984. In this essay*
*Baldwin takes a hard look at what an immigrant gives up and takes on in order to*
*become white.* From James Baldwin, "On Being White and Other Lies,"
originally published in *Essence* in 1984. Copyright (c) 1984 James Baldwin.
Source: James Baldwin Estate.

The crisis of leadership in the white community is remarkable—and
terrifying—because there is, in fact, no white community.

This may seem an enormous statement—and it is. I'm willing to be
challenged. I'm also willing to attempt to spell it out.

My frame of reference is, of course, America, or that portion of the
North American continent that calls itself America. And this means I
am speaking, essentially, of the European vision of the world—or
more precisely, perhaps, the European vision of the universe. It is a
vision as remarkable for what it pretends to include as for what it
remorselessly diminishes, demolishes or leaves totally out of
account.

There is, for example at least, in principle—an Irish community:
here, there, anywhere, or, more precisely, Belfast, Dublin and Boston. There is a German community: both sides of Berlin, Bavaria,
and Yorkville. There is an Italian community: Rome, Naples, the
Bank of the Holy Ghost and Mulberry Street. And there is a Jewish
community, stretching from Jerusalem to California to New York.
There are English communities. There are French communities.
There are Swiss consortiums. There are Poles: in Warsaw (where
they would like us to be friends) and in Chicago (where because
they are white we are enemies). There are, for that matter, Indian
restaurants and Turkish baths. There is the underworld—the poor
(to say nothing of those who intend to become rich) are always with
us—but this does not describe a community. It bears terrifying witness to what happened to everyone who got here, and paid the price
of the ticket. The price was to become "white." No one was white
before he/she came to America. It took generations, and a vast
amount of coercion, before this became a white country.

It is probable that it is the Jewish community—or more accurately,
perhaps, its remnants—that in America has paid the highest and
most extraordinary price for becoming white. For the Jews came

here from countries where they were not white, and they came here, in part, because they were not white; and incontestably—in the eyes of the Black American (and not only in those eyes) American Jews have opted to become white, and this is how they operate. It was ironical to hear, for example, former Israeli prime minister Menachem Begin declare some time ago that "the Jewish people bow only to God" while knowing that the state of Israel is sustained by a blank check from Washington. Without further pursuing the implication of this mutual act of faith, one is nevertheless aware that the Black Presence, here, can scarcely hope—at least, not yet—to halt the slaughter in South Africa.

And there is a reason for that.

America became white—the people who, as they claim, "settled" the country became white—because of the necessity of denying the Black presence, and justifying the Black subjugation. No community can be based on such a principle—or, in other words, no community can be established on so genocidal a lie. White men—from Norway, for example, where they were Norwegians—became white: by slaughtering the cattle, poisoning the wells, torching the houses, massacring Native Americans, raping Black women.

This moral erosion has made it quite impossible for those who think of themselves as white in this country to have any moral authority at all—privately, or publicly. The multitudinous bulk of them sit, stunned, before their TV sets, swallowing garbage that they know to be garbage, and—in a profound and unconscious effort to justify this torpor that disguises a profound and bitter panic—pay a vast amount of attention to athletics: even though they know that the football player (the Son of the Republic, their sons!) is merely another aspect of the money-making scheme. They are either relieved or embittered by the presence of the Black boy on the team. I do not know if they remember how long and hard they fought to keep him off it. I know that they do not dare have any notion of the price Black people (mothers and fathers) paid and pay. They do not want to know the meaning, or face the shame, of what they compelled—out of what they took as the necessity of being white—Joe Louis or Jackie Robinson or Cassius Clay (aka Muhammad Ali) to pay. I know that they, themselves, would not have liked to pay it.

There has never been a labor movement in this country, the proof being the absence of a Black presence in the so-called father-to-son unions. There are, perhaps, some niggers in the window; but Blacks have no power in the labor unions.

Just so does the white community, as a means of keeping itself white, elect, as they imagine, their political (!) representatives. No nation in the world, including England, is represented by so stunning a pantheon of the relentlessly mediocre. I will not name names—I will leave that to you.

But this cowardice, this necessity of justifying a totally false identity and of justifying what must be called a genocidal history, has placed everyone now living into the hands of the most ignorant and powerful people the world has ever seen: And how did they get that way?

By deciding that they were white. By opting for safety instead of life. By persuading themselves that a Black child's life meant nothing compared with a white child's life. By abandoning their children to the things white men could buy. By informing their children that Black women, Black men and Black children had no human integrity that those who call themselves white were bound to respect. And in this debasement and definition of Black people, they debased and defamed themselves.

And have brought humanity to the edge of oblivion: because they think they are white. Because they think they are white, they do not dare confront the ravage and the lie of their history. Because they think they are white, they cannot allow themselves to be tormented by the suspicion that all men are brothers. Because they think they are white, they are looking for, or bombing into existence, stable populations, cheerful natives and cheap labor. Because they think they are white, they believe, as even no child believes, in the dream of safety. Because they think they are white, however vociferous they may be and however multitudinous, they are as speechless as Lot's wife—looking backward, changed into a pillar of salt.

However—! White being, absolutely, a moral choice (for there *are* no white people), the crisis of leadership for those of us whose identity has been forced, or branded, as Black is nothing new. We—who were not Black before we got here either, who were defined as Black by the slave trade—have paid for the crisis of leadership in the white community for a very long time, and have resoundingly, even when we face the worst about ourselves, survived, and triumphed over it. If we had not survived and triumphed, there would not be a Black American alive.

And the fact that we are still here—even in suffering, darkness, danger, endlessly defined by those who do not dare define, or even confront, themselves—is the key to the crisis in white leadership. The past informs us of various kinds of people—criminals, adventurers and saints, to say nothing, of course, of popes—but it is the Black condition, and only that, which informs us concerning white people. It is a terrible paradox, but those who believed that they could control and define Black people divested themselves of the power to control and define themselves.

## Exercises: What's in a White Life?

The exercises given at the end of each section describe the activities best performed as a group. However, you can also do them by yourself. If you will be participating in a group, you may want to look over the exercises now to have time to reflect on the activities and your answers ahead of time.

The first section exercises consist of activities designed for taking the examination of whiteness to a personal level. The readings challenged the white acceptance of "whiteness" as invisible and unremarkable, portraying it as a complex, cultural condition. Now it's time to start examining whiteness in your own life.

### Social Geography

Race has an enormous impact in formative years. Yet, for white people, their own race is often invisible and unexamined. Social geography looks at the way race shapes the daily environments of both white people and people of color—at home, in school, when shopping or playing, visiting friends or family. By looking at where you grew up—maybe one neighborhood or many of them if your family moved frequently—you can begin to understand how race influenced your experiences, environment, and interactions.

Form a small group and share answers to the following questions:

- How do you describe your race or ethnicity?

- Where did you grow up?

- How would you describe the racial makeup of where you grew up? Be specific. Was your immediate neighborhood mixed? Your school? The grocery store? What do you mean by "mixed"?

- Did you have any relationships with people of a different race growing up? Did you interact with people of a different race? Did you see people of a different race? Try to remember all kinds of interactions from teacher to shop clerk to dentist.

- Were there any racial boundaries you were aware of growing up? For example, you were told to stay away from a certain neighborhood or somehow your family conveyed that you don't play with "those kind of people."

Don't forget to refer back to your previous notes on page 13. The above very specific questions will probably bring up more memories, as will hearing from other members of the group.

### When Are You White?

Given how elusive whiteness is, it is difficult to talk about. Lise Funderburg came up with a question she felt bypassed the elusive complexity and allowed the person responding to answer according to his or her own understanding of "whiteness." That question is simply, "When are you white?" For her own thoughts on the question and those of a few of the people she interviewed, see "When Are You White?" on page 23.

Choose a partner and interview each other by asking "When are you white?" If the person being interviewed stops talking, ask the question again. Do not ask any other questions or discuss the response. Allow two or three minutes per person. After exploring this question with your partner, discuss your responses and make some notes on what came up for both of you.

*Notes* _____

_____

_____

_____

_____

_____

_____

_____

_____

_____

_____

_____

_____

_____

# Section II

## *WHITE PRIVILEGE*

## Is Whiteness an Advantage?

Privilege is often hard to talk about. Most of those who are white don't see themselves as being treated special; they don't feel privileged. When white people hear the words "white privilege," defensiveness is often a first reaction, followed by fear that something is going to be taken away.   But white people need to examine the benefits to being white in this culture if they ever hope to experience diverse community. The basis of any diversity work or multicultural sensitivity for white people has to be a recognition of white privilege.

There are many ordinary ways that white people benefit from being white every day. And there are many cultural and institutional forces arrayed against those who try to make these privileges visible. We need to find ways to talk about white privilege so that it doesn't work as an invisible factor undermining efforts toward inclusivity and improved interracial relationships, both at work and in social gatherings.

Along with the very real advantages white people realize from white privilege, there is also a serious down side. As you begin to recognize the ways in which white privilege limits the lives of white people and cuts them off from the full range of human experience, you'll see how white privilege is more than a personal issue, but is key to understanding what brought us to the fragmented, violent, frightening, and racially divided society we live in today.

## Readings: Defining White Privilege

The readings include narratives of personal experience and analytic essays. They all challenge us to consider how white people benefit from being white—often in unexpected ways.

- In "White Privilege: Unpacking the Invisible Knapsack" Peggy McIntosh describes how she came to understand her own white privilege and provides a list of examples of common white privileges.

- In an excerpt from "The More I Like Flies" by Reginald McKnight, a young African-American man responds to the question "What's so great about being white?"

- In "Whiteness as Social Club" we've collected a sampling from *Race Traitor*, edited by Noel Ignatiev and John Garvey, which contains theories on the social and political construction of whiteness and the allure of white privilege in maintaining a racist system.

- Taking inventory of his life, in "Unearned Benefits," Robert Jenson lists all the ways in which being white smoothed his path through life.

## White Privilege: Unpacking the Invisible Knapsack

*"White Privilege: Unpacking the Invisible Knapsack," by Peggy McIntosh is the consummate white-privilege primer. Peggy McIntosh is Associate Director of the Wellesley College Center for Research on Women. This essay is adapted from her working paper, "White Privilege: Unpacking the Invisible Knapsack" adapted from "White Privelege and Male Privilege: A Personal Account of Coming to See Correspondences Through Work in Women's Studies," 1988.* Copyright (c) *1988* by Peggy McIntosh. May not be reprinted without permission of the author, Wellesley Centers for Women, Tel 781-283-2520, Fax: 781-283-2504.

Through work to bring materials from Women's Studies into the rest of the curriculum, I have often noticed men's unwillingness to grant that they are over-privileged, even though they may grant that women are disadvantaged. They may say they will work to improve women's status, in the society, the university, or the curriculum, but they can't or won't support the idea of lessening men's. Denials which amount to taboos surround the subject of advantages which men gain from women's disadvantages. These denials protect male privilege from being fully acknowledged, lessened or ended.

Thinking through unacknowledged male privilege as a phenomenon, I realized that since hierarchies in our society are interlocking, there was most likely a phenomenon of white privilege which was similarly denied and protected. As a white person, I realized I had been taught about racism as something which puts others at a disadvantage, but had been taught not to see one of its corollary aspects, white privilege, which puts me at an advantage.

I think whites are carefully taught not to recognize white privilege, as males are taught not to recognize male privilege. So I have begun in an untutored way to ask what it is like to have white privilege. I have come to see white privilege as an invisible package of unearned assets which I can count on cashing in each day, but about which I was 'meant' to remain oblivious. White privilege is like an invisible weightless knapsack of special provisions, maps, passports, codebooks, visas, clothes, tools and blank checks.

Describing white privilege makes one newly accountable. As we in Women's Studies work to reveal male privilege and ask men to give up some of their power, so one who writes about having white privilege must ask, "Having described it, what will I do to lessen or end it?"

After I realized the extent to which men work from a base of unacknowledged privilege, I understood that much of their oppressiveness was unconscious. Then I remembered the frequent charges from women of color that white women whom they encounter are oppressive. I began to understand why we are justly seen as oppressive, even when we don't see ourselves that way. I began to count the ways in which I enjoy unearned skin privilege and have been conditioned into oblivion about its existence.

My schooling gave me no training in seeing myself as an oppressor, as an unfairly advantaged person, or as a participant in a damaged culture. I was taught to see myself as an individual whose moral state depended on her individual moral will. My schooling followed the pattern my colleague Elizabeth Minnich has pointed out: whites are taught to think of their lives as morally neutral, normative and average, and also ideal, so that when we work to benefit others, this is seen as work which will allow "them" to be more like "us."

I decided to try to work on myself at least by identifying some of the daily effects of white privilege in my life. I have chosen those conditions which I think in my case attach *somewhat more to skin-color privilege* than to class, religion, ethnic status, or geographical location, though of course all these other factors are intricately intertwined. As far as I can see, my African American co-workers, friends and acquaintances with whom I come into daily or frequent contact in this particular time, place, and line of work cannot count on most of these conditions.

1. I can if I wish arrange to be in the company of people of my race most of the time.

2. If I should need to move, I can be pretty sure of renting or purchasing housing in an area which I can afford and in which I would want to live.

3. I can be pretty sure that my neighbors in such a location will be neutral or pleasant to me.

4. I can go shopping alone most of the time, pretty well assured that I will not be followed or harassed.

5. I can turn on the television or open to the front page of the paper and see people of my race widely represented.

6. When I am told about our national heritage or about "civilization" I am shown that people of my color made it what it is.

7. I can be sure that my children will be given curricular materials that testify to the existence of their race.

8. If I want to, I can be pretty sure of finding a publisher for this piece on white privilege.

9. I can go into a music shop and count on finding the music of my race represented, into a supermarket and find the staple foods which fit with my cultural traditions, into a hairdresser's shop and find someone who can cut my hair.

10. Whether I use checks, credit cards, or cash, I can count on my skin color not to work against the appearance of financial reliability.

11. I can arrange to protect my children most of the time from people who might not like them.

12. I can swear, or dress in second hand clothes, or not answer letters, without having people attribute these choices to the bad morals, the poverty, or the illiteracy of my race.

13. I can speak in public to a powerful male group without putting my race on trial.

14. I can do well in a challenging situation without being called a credit to my race.

15. I am never asked to speak for all the people of my racial group.

16. I can remain oblivious of the language and customs of persons of color who constitute the world's majority without feeling in my culture any penalty for such oblivion.

17. I can criticize our government and talk about how much I fear its policies and behavior without being seen as a cultural outsider.

18. I can be pretty sure that if I ask to talk to the "person in charge," I will be facing a person of my race.

19. If a traffic cop pulls me over or if the IRS audits my tax return, I can be sure I haven't been singled out because of my race.

20. I can easily buy posters, postcards, picture books, greeting cards, dolls, toys, and children's magazines featuring people of my race.

21. I can go home from most meetings of organizations I belong to feeling somewhat tied in, rather than isolated, out-of-place, out-numbered, unheard, held at a distance, or feared.

22. I can take a job with an affirmative action employer without having co-workers on the job suspect that I got it because of race.

23. I can choose public accommodation without fearing that people of my race cannot get in or will be mistreated in the places I have chosen.

24. I can be sure that if I need legal or medical help, my race will not work against me.

25. If my day, week, or year is going badly, I need not ask of each negative episode or situation whether it has racial overtones.

26. I can choose blemish cover or bandages in "flesh" color and have them more or less match my skin.

I repeatedly forgot each of the realizations on this list until I wrote it down. For me white privilege has turned out to be an elusive and fugitive subject. The pressure to avoid it is great, for in facing it I must give up the myth of meritocracy. If these things are true, this is not such a free country, ones life is not what one makes it; many doors open for certain people through no virtues of their own.

In unpacking this invisible knapsack of white privilege, I have listed conditions of daily experience which I once took for granted. Nor did I think of any of these perquisites as bad for the holder. I now think that we need a more finely differentiated taxonomy of privilege, for some of these varieties are only what one would want for everyone in a just society, and others give license to be ignorant, oblivious, arrogant and destructive.

I see a pattern running through the matrix of white privilege, a pattern of assumptions which were passed on to me as a white person. There was one main piece of cultural turf; it was my own turf, and I was among those who could control the turf. *My skin color was an asset, for any move I was educated to want to make.* I could think of myself at belonging in major ways, and of making social systems work for me. I could freely disparage, fear, neglect, or be oblivious to anything outside of the dominant cultural forms. Being of the main culture, I could also criticize it fairly freely.

In proportion as my racial group was being made confident, comfortable, and oblivious, other groups were likely being made unconfident, uncomfortable, and alienated. Whiteness protected me from many kinds of hostility, distress, and violence, which I was being subtly trained to visit in turn upon people of color.

For this reason, the word "privilege" now seems to me misleading. We usually think of privilege as being a favored state, whether earned or conferred by birth or luck. Yet some of the conditions I have described here work to systematically overempower certain groups. Such privilege simply *confers dominance* because of ones race or sex.

I want, then, to distinguish between earned strength and unearned power conferred systemically. Power from unearned privilege can look like strength when it is in fact permission to escape or to dominate. But not all of the privileges on my list are inevitably damaging. Some, like the expectation that neighbors will be decent to you, or that your race will not count against you in court, should be the norm in a just society. Others, like the privilege to ignore less powerful people, distort the humanity of the holders as well as the ignored groups.

We might at least start by distinguishing between positive advantages which we can work to spread, and negative types of advantages which unless rejected will always reinforce our present hierarchies. For example, the feeling that one belongs within the human circle, as Native Americans say, should not be seen as privilege for a few. Ideally it is an *unearned entitlement*. At present, since only a few have it, it is an *unearned advantage* for them. This paper results from a process of coming to see that some of the power which I originally saw as attendant on being a human being in the U.S. consisted in unearned advantage and conferred dominance. I have met very few men who are truly distressed about systemic, unearned male advantage and conferred dominance. And so one question for me and others like me is whether we will be like them, or whether we will get truly distressed, even outraged, about unearned race advantage and conferred dominance and if so, what we will do to lessen them. In any case, we need to do more work in identifying how they actually affect our daily lives. Many, perhaps most, of our white students in the U.S. think that racism doesn't affect them because they are not people of color; they do not see "whiteness" as a racial identity. In addition, since race and sex are not the only advantaging systems at work, we need similarly to examine the daily experience of having age advantage, or ethnic advantage, or physical ability, or advantage related to nationality, religion, or sexual orientation.

Difficulties and dangers surrounding the task of finding parallels are many. Since racism, sexism, and heterosexism are not the same, the advantaging associated with them should not be seen as the same. In addition, it is hard to disentangle aspects of unearned advantage which rest more on social class, economic class, race, religion, sex and ethnic identity than on other factors. Still, all of the oppressions are interlocking, as the Combahee River Collective Statement of 1977 continues to remind us eloquently.

One factor seems clear about all of the interlocking oppressions. They take both active forms which we can see and embedded forms which as a member of the dominant group one is taught not to see. In my class and place, I did not see myself as a racist because I was taught to recognize racism only in individual acts of meanness by members of my group, never in invisible systems conferring unsought racial dominance on my group from birth.

Disapproving of the systems won't be enough to change them. I was taught to think that racism could end if white individuals changed their attitudes. [But] a "white" skin in the United States opens many doors for whites whether or not we approve of the way dominance has been conferred on us. Individual acts can palliate, but cannot end, these problems.

To redesign social systems we need first to acknowledge their colossal unseen dimensions. The silences and denials surrounding privilege are the key political tool here. They keep the thinking about equality or equity incomplete, protecting unearned advantage and conferred dominance by making these taboo subjects. Most talk by whites about equal opportunity seems to me now to be about equal opportunity to try to get into a position of dominance while denying that *systems* of dominance exist.

It seems to me that obliviousness about white advantage, like obliviousness about male advantage, is kept strongly inculturated in the

United States so as to maintain the myth of meritocracy, the myth that democratic choice is equally available to all. Keeping most people unaware that freedom of confident action is there for just a small number of people props up those in power, and serves to keep power in the hands of the same groups that have most of it already.

Though systemic change takes many decades, there are pressing questions for me and I imagine for some others like me if we raise our daily consciousness on the perquisites of being light-skinned. What will we do with such knowledge? As we know from watching men, it is an open question whether we will choose to use unearned advantage to weaken hidden systems of advantage, and whether we will use any of our arbitrarily-awarded power to try to reconstruct, power systems on a broader base.

### *The More I Like Flies (excerpt)*

*In the short story, "The More I Like Flies" the narrator, a young African-American man is working as a bus boy with a rather obtuse, older white man. In this excerpt he answers one of his partner's endless questions.* Excerpt from "The More I Like Flies" from *White Boys*, 1999. Copyright (c) 1999 Henry Holt and Company. Source: Henry Holt and Company.

. . . But then, like from nowhere ol' Kelly, my partner, goes, "What's so great about bein goddam white?" Hello! I say to myself. There he goes. Good ol' Kelly. But I keep my mouth shut, naturally. No sense going into it. This is Kelly.

But still, I'm thinking, How about this, ya dope: Try walking down the street at night, minding your own besswax, and a white couple comes at you from the opposite way? and it's hot outside, so you're ambling, and it's not all that late, just blue black with a few stars, like you like it, and you're thinking about, say, nothing really, okay? and you don't even mind the water sprinklers spitting on your right side. And the crickets sound nice, don't they? Then when Ken and Barbie get within a half block of you they cut across the street like you're a hissing viper hellhound man, bristling with Uzis and hypodermic needles. You can barely keep yourself from hollering, *Oh come ooonnn, I gotta Korean girlfriend and my best buddy's white, and you people got to simply lay off renting so many goddam gangsta movies. Kumbaya, baby. I'm respectable.* Pin heads. What's so great about being white is you get to act like everybody else in the world is a scary monster.

### *Whiteness as a Social Club*

*A common theory attempting to explain racial inequalities in the U.S. views whiteness as a social construct. In the anthology* Race Traitor, *edited by Noel Ignatiev and John Garvey, whiteness is described as a "white club" whose members gain certain privileges. Looking at whiteness in this way can give us a new perspective on racial problems and help white people come to terms with white privilege. Here are some excerpts from* Race Traitor, *gathered to give you an overview of the theory.*

In the book's introduction, Noel Ignatiev writes:

> The white race is a historically constructed social formation—historically constructed because (like royalty) it is a product of some people's responses to historical circumstances; a social formation because it is a fact of society corresponding to no classification recognized by natural science.

> The white race cuts across ethnic and class lines. It is not coextensive with that portion of the population of European descent, since many of those classified as "colored" can trace some of their ancestry to Europe, while African, Asian, or American Indian blood flows through the veins of many considered white. Nor does membership in the white race imply wealth, since there are plenty of poor whites, as well as some people of wealth and comfort who are not white. (page 9)

There is plenty of historical evidence for the view that whiteness was a constructed category. For example, many immigrant groups now considered white where not so defined when they first arrived in the U.S. — Irish, Italian, and Jewish, for example. In "Immigrants and Whites," Ignatiev writes:

> At the turn of the century, an investigator into conditions in the steel industry, seeking employment on a blast furnace, was informed that "only Hunkies work on those jobs, they're too damn dirty and too damn hot for a 'white' man." Around the same time, a West Coast construction boss was asked, "You don't call an Italian a white man?" "No, sir," came the reply, "an Italian is a dago." Odd though this usage may seem today, it was at one time fairly common. According to one historian, "in all sections native-born and northern European laborers called themselves 'white men' to distinguish themselves from the Southern Europeans they worked beside." I have even heard of a time when it was said in the Pacific Northwest logging industry that no whites worked in these woods, just a bunch of Swedes.

Today, if we are considered white, we probably never consciously chose our membership in the "white club." In the introduction, Ignatiev writes:

It is our faith ... that the majority of so-called whites in this country are neither deeply nor consciously committed to white supremacy; like most human beings in most times and places, they would do the right thing if it were convenient. As did their counterparts before the Civil War, most go along with a system that disturbs them because the consequences of challenging it are terrifying. They close their eyes to what is happening around them, because it is easier not to know. (pg 12)

If whiteness is a social construct, does that mean it can be undone? The writers in *Race Traitor* argue that those defined as white can renounce their membership in the white club and that if enough people do so, the system of white supremacy will no longer work. In "Richmond Journal" Edward Peeples writes of his experience as a young boy during World War II. His family owned a small grocery store where he helped out after school. Bread was in very short supply and his father saved the bread for his white customers, keeping it under the counter and telling any black customer who asked for bread that he didn't have any. Peeples followed these guidelines until one day a black woman walked into the store and asked for bread:

For perhaps the first time in my brief life I saw in her no mythical figure invented and embellished by white fear and ignorance. Rather ... I perceived a person who, like everyone else I knew, just wanted to get through the burdensome effects of this, the last great war in behalf of freedom and democracy. ...

She repeated her request with emphasis—"And a loaf of bread!" Her words broke my concentration. "Uh ... Yea," I said and reached under the counter and brought out a loaf of bread...

My imagination followed her all the way home where I saw her trudge into her house, drop her grocery bag onto the kitchen table in exhaustion, and then flop down onto her living room sofa—as I had seen my own mother do so often after a hard day's work. And in my mind, I saw her young son race into the kitchen, reach into the grocery bag, lift out the bread in the dark blue wrapper, rip open the end of it, pull out a fresh fluffy piece of white bread, and eat it with great singularity of pleasure.

From that time on, my father would periodically ask me why was the bread always sold out so early when I was out in the front of the store. I told him that we were having a lot more white customers coming in now.

In writing of her own life in "Manifesto of a Dead Daughter," Patricia Eakins describes her experience in rebelling against her white suburban home life as a girl and finding herself in a black urban setting. Reflecting back on her experiences, she says:

> To me, "white" stood for and stands for not so much a degree of pigmentation as a set of attitudes that takes privilege as an exclusive right. We are all of us always members of some groups that can or do oppress others. To be "white" means to be insensitive to the possibilities for oppression within one's self, therefore out-of-touch, for opportunistic reasons, with who one is and who others are. If "white" mean all-inclusive, like white the color of light containing all colors, then "white" would be a term of love and life. But the "white" I'm talking about is a whiteness of exclusion, an absence of color, an absence of responsibility and self-awareness. Whiteness is a death trip. And that the attempt to break out of it is an attempt to gain life.

> To be a person of color means to feel with one's heart that one is mortal among mortals; one takes one's place in a matrix that relationally defines and redefines one's place in one's culture. To be a person of color is to acknowledge that we are hurt as well as blessed in our vulnerability. No one was born to be victim, scapegoat, or mule, Together we grow toward the bright light that contains all color, the light that is wisdom. Each of us reflects a luster that is part of the full spectrum of human possibility, pleasure, creativity, generosity, faith, and beauty.

## Benefits of Unearned Privilege

*What would a level playing field really look like? Robert Jenson writes that white people need to acknowledge the benefits of unearned privilege. The article was distributed by the Dawn/LAT-WP News Service, and the copyright is held by the Baltimore Sun.*

Here's what white privilege sounds like: I'm sitting in my University of Texas office, talking to a very bright and very conservative white student about affirmative action in college admissions, which he opposes and I support. The student says he wants a level playing field with no unearned advantages for anyone. I ask him whether he thinks that being white has advantages in the United States. Have either of us, I ask, ever benefited from being white in a world run mostly by white people? Yes, he concedes, there is something real and tangible we could call white privilege. So, if we live in a world of white privilege—unearned white privilege—how does that affect your notion of a level playing field? I asked. He paused for a moment and said, "That really doesn't matter."
That statement, I suggested to him, reveals the ultimate white privilege: the privilege to acknowledge that you have unearned privilege but to ignore what it means.

That exchange led me to rethink the way I talk about race and racism with students. It drove home the importance of confronting the dirty secret that we white people carry around with us every day: in a world of white privilege, some of what we have is unearned. I think much of both the fear and anger that comes up around discussions of affirmative action has its roots in that secret. So these days, my goal is to talk openly and honestly about white supremacy and white privilege.

White privilege, like any social phenomenon, is complex. In a white supremacist culture, all white people have privilege, whether or not they are overtly racist themselves. There are general patterns, but such privilege plays out differently depending on context and other aspects of one's identity (in my case, being male gives me other kinds of privilege). Rather than try to tell others how white privilege has played out in their lives, I talk about how it has affected me.

I am as white as white gets in this country. I am of northern European heritage and I was raised in North Dakota, one of the whitest states in the country. I grew up in a virtually all-white world surrounded by racism, both personal and institutional. Because I didn't live near a reservation, I didn't even have exposure to the state's only numerically significant nonwhite population, American Indians. I have struggled to resist that racist training and the racism of my culture. I like to think I have changed, even though I routinely trip over the lingering effects of that internalized racism and the institutional racism around me. But no matter how much I "fix" myself, one thing never changes—I walk through the world with white privilege.

What does that mean? Perhaps most importantly, when I seek admission to a university, apply for a job, or hunt for an apartment, I don't look threatening. Almost all of the people evaluating me look like me—they are white. They see in me a reflection of themselves—and in a racist world, that is an advantage. I smile. I am white. I am one of them. I am not dangerous. Even when I voice critical opinions, I am cut some slack. After all, I'm white.

My flaws also are more easily forgiven because I am white. Some complain that affirmative action has meant the university is saddled with mediocre minority professors. I have no doubt there are minority faculty who are mediocre, though I don't know very many. As Henry Louis Gates Jr. once pointed out, if affirmative action policies were in place for the next hundred years, it's possible that at the end of that time the university could have as many mediocre minority professors as it has mediocre white professors. That isn't meant as an insult to anyone, but it's a simple observation that white privilege has meant that scores of second-rate white professors have slid through the system because their flaws were overlooked out of solidarity based on race, as well as on gender, class and ideology.

Some people resist the assertions that the United States is still a bitterly racist society and that the racism has real effects on real people. But white folks have long cut other white folks a break. I know, because I am one of them. I am not a genius—as I like to say, I'm not the sharpest knife in the drawer. I have been teaching full time for six years and I've published a reasonable amount of scholarship. Some of it is the unexceptional stuff one churns out to get tenure, and some of it, I would argue, is worth reading. I worked hard, and I like to think that I'm a fairly decent teacher. Every once in a while, I leave my office at the end of the day feeling like I really accomplished something. When I cash my paycheck, I don't feel guilty. But, all that said, I know I did not get where I am by merit alone. I benefited from among other things, white privilege. That doesn't mean that I don't deserve my job, or that if I weren't white I would never have gotten the job. It means simply that all through my life, I have soaked up benefits for being white.

All my life I have been hired for jobs by white people. I was accepted for graduate school by white people. And I was hired for a teaching position by the predominantly white University of Texas, headed by a white president, in a college headed by a white dean and in a department with a white chairman that at the time had one nonwhite tenured professor. I have worked hard to get where I am, and I work hard to stay there. But to feel good about myself and my work, I do not have to believe that "merit" as defined by white people in a white country, alone got me here. I can acknowledge that in addition to all that hard work, I got a significant boost from white privilege.

At one time in my life, I would not have been able to say that, because I needed to believe that my success in life was due solely to my individual talent and effort. I saw myself as the heroic American, the rugged individualist. I was so deeply seduced by the culture's mythology that I couldn't see the fear that was binding me to those myths. Like all white Americans, I was living with the fear that maybe I didn't really deserve my success, that maybe luck and privilege had more to do with it than brains and hard work. I was afraid I wasn't heroic or rugged, that I wasn't special.

I let go of some of that fear when I realized that, indeed, I wasn't special, but that I was still me. What I do well, I still can take pride in, even when I know that the rules under which I work in are stacked to my benefit. Until we let go of the fiction that people have complete control over their fate—that we can will ourselves to be anything we choose—then we will live with that fear. White privilege is not something I get to decide whether I want to keep. Every time I walk into a store at the same time as a black man and the security guard follows him and leaves me alone to shop, I am benefiting from white privilege. There is not space here to list all the ways in which white privilege plays out in our daily lives, but it is clear that I will carry this privilege with me until the day white supremacy is erased from this society.

## Reflecting: Making White Privilege Visible

After reading "White Privilege: Unpacking the Invisible Knapsack" by Peggy McIntosh, answer the following four questions.

1. Which privileges of those that McIntosh lists in her article especially resonate with you?

_____

_____

_____

_____

_____

_____

_____

_____

2. What are five ways, not listed in the article, that white people benefit from being white? For example, "If I as a white person don't get to rent an apartment I like, I don't think it's because I am white."

_____

_____

_____

_____

_____

_____

_____

3. What are five ways in which white people are hurt by white privilege? For example, "White people are deprived of a well-rounded education in that their education includes almost nothing about the rich history and cultures of the America's, Asia, and Africa."

_____

_____

_____

_____

_____

_____

_____

_____

4. What are some privileges you have benefited from that would be difficult to surrender.

_____

_____

_____

_____

_____

_____

_____

_____

_____

## Exercises: Grappling with Privilege

Talking about white privilege is extremely difficult, especially for white people who often respond with defensiveness, anger, and denial. In the following exercises, you will look for non-judgemental ways of discussing how white people benefit from being white. You will also attempt to understand why whites so often react poorly when hearing about white privilege from a person of color. Finally, in looking deeper into white privilege, you will try to see the ways in which those who benefit are also hurt by it.

### *How Do We Talk About White Privilege*

Form a group to discuss the following questions:

- How is a white person talking about white privilege seen or heard by white friends and colleagues?

- How is a person of color talking about white privilege seen by white friends and colleagues?

- How can you create a climate in which a person of color enumerating white privileges can have as much credibility and appear as rationally analytical as a white person doing so?

*Notes* _____

_____

_____

_____

_____

_____

_____

_____

_____

_____

_____

_____

_____

_____

_____

### Is There a Flip Side to White Privilege?

Acknowledging and enumerating white privileges often leads to a deeper understanding of what is necessary to support the system that maintains these privileges. For example, as shown in the section "Whiteness," racial barriers often keep people apart, so although white privilege may allow white people to live in a desirable suburb, they are denied meaningful interaction with people of color. As a result they have no realistic images of people of color, lose the richness of diversity, and don't get to hear the full story on many current issues of concern. Ultimately, many who benefit most from white privilege end up living in fear of those who benefit least from an unjust system.

In a group, brainstorm ways in which whites are hurt by white privilege and then consider the results. For example, as white people we live without diversity; we are enmeshed with injustice; we accept violence as a way of life.

_____

_____

_____

_____

_____

_____

_____

_____

_____

_____

# Section III
## *VOICES*

## Hearing the Voices of People of Color

White people often find themselves living in an all-white world and thus know very little about the lives of people of color from personal experience. Many of the images or stories of people of color are passed through distorted history or mainstream media and do not reflect people of color's original experiences or perceptions. Without personal relationships and with biased information, this leaves whites with stereotypes and misconceptions about people of color.

Even when personal interactions between white people and people of color occur, both sides may unconsciously filter what they see and hear through preconceptions, losing the possibility of authentic communication and making faulty assessments. In other words, we often fail to understand and at the same time feel we are being misinterpreted.

In this section we look at how white privilege and lack of information come together to impede interracial communication. You will begin by examining the belief systems you were raised with, that taught you about people who were different from you, noticing that your interior feelings and beliefs about race are shaped by the cultural and institutional forces of racism. You will then look at ways that you can remedy your lack of accurate information about those different from you, for example, by reading a novel by a Chicana or attending the screening of a movie produced and directed by Native Americans. In essence, you will be asked to challenge the choices you make in your life that may perpetuate the dominance of the white world in your entertainment, your travels, your daily activities.

Communication requires two actions—giving voice and hearing. When communication fails, some feel unheard and others feel no one will talk to them. We've all had experiences of feeling unheard. Or we know we have ways to keep ourselves from hearing things we don't want to hear. By paying attention to how you feel in those situations you can try to recognize times when you are retreating from true communication.

White people often act on misperceptions and as a result deliver messages to people of color that are patronizing or that maintain white dominance. For example, people of color are frequently told by white people that they "think everything is about racism", or are "taking things too seriously, that's not what I meant." When we can really hear each other's voices, instead of challenging each other's perceptions, we can ask "Tell me more. I didn't see it that way."

## Readings: Expanding Our World

The readings address the importance of voice—in terms of both content and language. Several of these reading may really challenge your listening abilities.

- In "Forked Tongues" Aurora Levins Morales describes writing as a form of cultural and spiritual self-defense for U.S. Puerto Ricans.

- An excerpt from *La Maravilla* by Alfredo Véa, Jr. talks about what white people owe to black and Mexican voices.

- In "Notes from a Fragmented Daughter" Elena Tajima Creef uses storytelling to articulate who she is.

- A poet laments the necessity of writing political poems in "Poem For The Young White Man Who Asked Me How I, An Intelligent, Well-Read Person, Could Believe In the War Between Races" by Lorna Dee Cervantes.

As you are reading, mark a few paragraphs that especially resonate with you. Try reading these paragraphs aloud to a friend and then talking about what the reading means to you.

### *Forked Tongues: On Not Speaking Spanish (excerpt)*

*Aurora Levins Morales describes the necessity from which U.S. Puerto Rican authors write, the necessity to be seen through their own eyes rather than through the lens of racism. This excerpt is part of a larger essay that also describes the "delicious blend" of English and Spanish plus words from many cultures that become the voice of diasporic Puerto Ricans.* From Aurora Levins Morales, "Forked Tongues" from *Medicine Stories: History, Culture, and the Politics of Integrity,* 1998, pp. 61-62. Copyright (c) South End Press. Reprinted with permission of South End Press.

To understand what we prose writers of the diaspora are doing, it is necessary to know why and how we are writing. Storytelling is a basic human activity with which we simultaneously make and understand the world and our place in it.

The world in which U.S. Puerto Rican writing takes place, the context that most profoundly determines its form, is racism. Racism firmly rooted in class, in both the original class identities of those who migrated and in the enforcement of a persistent poverty on the diaspora community. Unrelenting racism that permeates our daily lives in all its forms, from brutality and humiliation at the hands of the police, schools and other institutions to the most subtle ways of making us disappear as human beings. Our history is stolen from us. We are stripped of our names. We are made into caricatures in a burlesque written by those who despise us or know nothing at all of us.

So the first and most important thing to understand is that we write from necessity; that our writing is a form of cultural and spiritual self-defense. To live surrounded by a popular culture in which we do not appear is a form of spiritual erasure that leaves us vulnerable to all the assaults a society can commit against those it does not recognize. Not to be recognized, not to find oneself in history, or in film, or on television, or in books, or in popular songs, or in what is studied at school leads to the psychic disaster of ceasing to recognize oneself. Our literature is documentation of an existence that doesn't matter a damn to those in charge. And like the forged passports of my paternal Jewish relatives, from time to time it saves our lives.

This is why we write: to see ourselves on the page. To confirm our presence. To clear a space where we can examine the lives we live, not as the sexy girlfriends, petty crooks and crime victims of TV cop shows, and not as statistical profiles in which hardship, bravery and resourcefullness lose all personality, but in our own physical and emotional reality. Where we can pull apart and explore this complex relationship we have with the island of our origins and kinship, and this vast many-peopled country in which we are writing a new chapter of Puerto Ricanhood. This necessity gives shape to our literature, to our urgent poetry of the streets, our ever-so-autobiographical fiction, our legends of collective identity. Most of what we write, we write under pressure.

## Short excerpt from *La Maravilla*

*In this excerpt from the novel* La Maravilla *by Alfredo Véa, Jr., Josephina, the protagonist's Mexican grandmother talks about what African-Americans have contributed to American culture.* Excerpt from *La Maravilla* by Alfredo Véa, Jr., 1994. Copyright (c) 1994 Dutton Press, an imprint of Penguin Putnam Inc. Source: Penguin Putnam Inc.

"Whites pass," Josephina had said, her finger in the boy's face.

"Whites go into the melting pot. Polish and Hungarians shorten their names, they cut the words that bind them to their own. Germans, French forget their languages, pronounce through their noses and disappear into the Twin Cities. Not los Negros or los Indios; or la Raza, the Mexicans," she said. "Tenemos la insignia." Josephina had touched her finger to her skin and then to the boy's to make her point.

"We have the badge, and if we didn't we'd make one. The Indians and the Raza have always had their language; the fountain of their cultura is right here or just across that so-called border in Mexico. The blacks, far from Africa, made theirs from the language they were forced to use, reshaped it." She moved her hands as if she were molding clay.

"They played and danced, they cried and worshiped with it. And because they were always separated from the whites, they separated themselves." She demonstrated by moving her hands apart.

"They said: 'We are always told how different we are, let's make it an act of will.' And they did. Imagine what American music would be without the blacks, the latinos."

It was the genealogy of Josephina's gospel.

"La verdad, it was the slaves who freed America," Abuela would say. "Now the whites are milking los Negros of their musica and their language."

Josephina would pull out her 78s or her new LPs for any group of kids that would listen. Often she would bribe them with food, then play her music while they ate.

"Listen to this, hijos. You hear what Jimmy Dorsey is doing here, right here with the trumpet section. Shit, the black bands were doing that fifteen years earlier. Listen to this."

She would clean her records carefully with her apron, then wind the record player violently before each selection.

"This is King Oliver, a genius," she would smile as she dropped the needle into the first groove of Stingaree Blues, "a genius. He died, you know, sweeping up a pool hall in Savannah, Georgia...."

### Notes from a Fragmented Daughter

*In "Notes from a Fragmented Daughter," Elena Tajima Creef gives us some snapshots of her life as the daughter of a Japanese war bride and American serviceman. Through her story we can see many of the stereotypes about Asian women and the confusion of being mixed race. Finally we see how she returns to herself through anger and truth-telling.* From Elena Tajima Creef, "Notes from a Fragmented Daughter" in *Making Face, Making Soul/Hacienda Caras: Creative and Critical Perspectives by Women of Color* edited by Gloria Anzaldúa, 1990, pp. 82-84. Copyright (c) 1990 Aunt Lute Books. Source: Aunt Lute Books.

## Some Personal Scenes

1. At an art gallery opening for local Asian American women artists, a tall white man in glasses, beard, and big hair bundled up into a ponytail hovers over a table full of sushi, chow mein, egg rolls, and teriyaki chicken. He looks at me awkwardly and attempts conversation. "Did you make any of the food? I notice you look kinda Asian."

2. Marion is half Chinese and half Japanese and I like the way his face looks. We sit and talk about what it means to have mixed backgrounds in a culture that can't tell Chinese apart from Japanese and where McDonald's still serves Shanghai Chicken McNuggets with teriyaki sauce.

3. I am fifteen and am sitting in the backseat of my best friend Doreen's Volkswagen Bug, when her uncle's new wife Clara climbs into the passenger seat and we are introduced. Clara speaks in tongues at the Ladies Prayer Meetings, and has seen angels in the sky through her Kodak Instamatic.

She turns to me and shouts in a thick New York accent, "So what are you studying?"

I say, "English."

She says, "Gee, your English is very good. How long have you been in this country?" I say, "All of my life."

She shouts, "Are you Chinese?" I say, "Japanese."

She says, "I admire your people very much!"

I smile and say, "Yes, and we are very good with our hands, too."

4. Katie Gonzales follows me around for one week at sixth grade summer camp, her left arm in a sling from a tetherball accident. "I'm gonna get you, you flat-faced chinaman." I want to tell her that I'm only half-Japanese, but the words stick in my mouth and instead, I call her a beaner and imagine I am twisting that left arm right off her brown skinny body.

5. Later, when I am thirteen, I bury my mother once and for all and decide to go Mexican. It makes a lot of sense. I am no longer Elena, I am now Elaina and I begin insisting I am Mexican wherever I go. With my long black hair, my sun-darkened skin, and my new name, I can pass and I am safe. For the next year, I obsessively hide my Japanese mother and deny my Japanese roots. No one is allowed to meet her. I do not let her answer the phone if I can help it, or go near the door if I can get there first. I sabotage the PTA's efforts to get her to come to their monthly meetings, and I conveniently get dates mixed up for "Open House." I live in fear that someone will find out that my mother is Japanese and spread it around the classroom like a dirty rumor. I love it when people ask if I am Español, because it is safe, because it means I do not stand out.

6. My mother and I are getting out of the car at Builder's Emporium when a young, ugly, straw-haired man gets out of his truck and shouts that my mother has stolen his parking space. She says she doesn't know what he's talking about and he tells her to shut up her slant-eyed face. My heart is pounding as we shop for light fixtures and nails but we never say a thing.

7. It is a dark, wet, rainy Santa Cruz night, and I go to see "Tampopo"—your basic Japanese noodle western—by myself. I am in a very good mood and allow a balding middle-aged man with a burgundy plum scarf tied around his neck to make conversation with me in the lobby.

"I really love Japanese films, almost as much as I love Asian girls! I'm going to Taiwan next month to meet this woman I've been corresponding with. I really prefer Oriental women to American because (he whispers) there are so many 'feminists' in this town. You are Asian, aren't you? Don't tell me let me guess. Japanese? Chinese? Hawaiian? Eurasian?"

Idiot. I am the daughter of a World War II Japanese war bride who met and married my North Carolinian hillbilly father one fine day in 1949 while she was hanging up the laundry to dry. Nine months out of the year, I pose as a doctoral student—a historian of consciousness; the rest of the time, I am your basic half-Japanese postmodernist gemini feminist existentialist would-be writer of bad one-act comedy revues, avid cat trainer, and closet reader of mademoiselle, cosmo, signs, diacritics, elle, tv guide, cultural critique, representations, people magazine, critical inquiry, national enquirer, feminist issues, house beautiful, architectural digest, country living, cat fancy, bird talk, mother jones, covert action, vogue, glamour, the new yorker, l.a. times, l. a. weekly, and sometimes penthouse forum.

So how do you like them apples, bub? If you come near me one more time with your touch-me-feel-you New Age Bagwan male sensitivity, I just may strangle you with the burgundy plum scarf you have tied around your neck.

## Deconstructing My Mother as the Other

The headlines blare: "They're Bringing Home Japanese Brides! Six thousand Americans in Japan have taken Japanese brides since 1945, and all the little Madam Butterflys are studying hamburgers, Hollywood and home on the range, before coming to live in the U.S.A."

Although she is not interviewed, my mother appears in one of the bright technicolor photographs in the January 19, 1952, issue of the *Saturday Evening Post*. She is the short one with the funny hairdo, hovering over an apple pie, smiling with her classmates in the American Red Cross "Brides' School" for Japanese Wives. While the article attempts to tell the postwar story of the Japanese war bride in general, it also tells the story of how my own American G.I. father met and married my Japanese mother in war-torn occupied Japan. It is, in essence, my own pictorial origin story.

There are over 45,000 Japanese women who married American servicemen after World War 11 and immigrated to the United States. I have been meeting and interviewing these women for the last few years for a collection of oral histories I hope to someday publish. I have been told over and over again by many of these women that they despise the name "war bride." There is something dirty and derogatory about this word, but rarely has anyone told me why. "Call us 'Shin Issei' (the New Immigrants)," they say. Or how about, "Japanese Wives of American Servicemen." Don't call us "war brides." They whisper, "It is not nice."

I am the daughter of a World War II Japanese war bride who met and married my white North Carolinan hillbilly father one fine day in 1949 while she was hanging up the laundry to dry.

There is no escaping this body made out of history,
war and peace,
two languages,
and two cultures.

My name is Elena June,
I am the youngest daughter of Chiyohi,
who is the only surviving daughter of Iso,
who was the daughter of the Mayor of Yokoze
and was the Village Beauty
born in the last century to a Japanese woman
whose name is now forgotten,
 but who lived in the Meiji era
and loved to tell ghost stories.

### Poem For The Young White Man Who Asked Me How I, An Intelligent, Well-Read Person, Could Believe In the War Between Races

*This poems compares the poet's dreamland with the reality of her life as a person of color.* From Lorna Dee Cervantes,"Poem For The Young White Man Who Asked Me How I, An Intelligent, Well-Read Person, Could Believe In the War Between Races" in EMPLUMADA, 1981, pp. 35-37. Copyright (c) 1981 University of Pittsburg Press. Source: University of Pittsburg Press.

In my land there are no distinctions.
The barbed wire politics of oppression
have been torn down long ago. The only reminder
of past battles, lost or won, is a slight
rutting in the fertile fields.

In my land
people write poems about love,
full of nothing but contented childlike syllables.
Everyone reads Russian short stories and weeps.
There are no boundaries.
There is no hunger, no
complicated famine or greed.

I am not a revolutionary.
I don't even like political poems.
Do you think I can believe in a war between races?
I can deny it. I can forget about it
when I'm safe,
living on my own continent of harmony
and home, but I am not
there.

I believe in revolution
because everywhere the crosses are burning,
sharp-shooting goose-steppers round every corner,
there are snipers in the schools...
(I know you don't believe this.
You think this is nothing but faddish exaggeration. But they
are not shooting at you.)

I'm marked by the color of my skin.
The bullets are discrete and designed to kill slowly.
They are aiming at my children.
These are facts.
Let me show you my wounds: my stumbling mind, my
"excuse me" tongue, and this
nagging preoccupation
with the feeling of not being good enough.

These bullets bury deeper than logic.

Outside my door
there is a real enemy
who hates me.

I am a poet
who yearns to dance on rooftops,
to whisper delicate lines about joy
and the blessings of human understanding.
I try. I go to my land, my tower of words and
bolt the door, but the typewriter doesn't fade out
the sounds of blasting and muffled outrage.
My own days bring me slaps on the face.
Every day I am deluged with reminders
that this is not
my land

and this is my land

I do not believe in the war between races

but in this country
there is war.

# Reflecting: Challenging Stereotypes

In an effort to examine the opinions and images you carry about people from various ethnic and racial groups, journal on the questions listed below. We have created eight groupings. Answer the questions about one group at a time, breaking the exercise into several days.

Try to let yourself drop into the questions—don't let your mind stop you from examining whatever surfaces, even if you know it's "bad" or feel embarrassed by your own thoughts. None of us chose to be exposed to racial stereotypes. By examining what we carry—unwillingly—within, we can begin to challenge the power these twisted images and voices have over our actions.

The groups are arbitrary and designed simply as a means to help you focus on detail and specifics. Notice that the collective categories often lump together many very different nationalities

- Asian-American and Asian Pacific Islander (for example, Chinese-American, Japanese-American, Filipino-American, East Indian–American, Hawaiian)
- African-American
- Arab-American
- Chicano, La Raza, Puerto Rican, Hispanic, Latino
- Mixed race
- Native-American, Aleut
- White (for example, Anglo-American, Irish-American, Swedish-American)
- Jewish-American (although included in white, Jewish-American is separated out here due to anti-semitism; also, there are Asian, Latino, and African Jews)

Ask the following questions of each group above and, using the following blank pages, journal on what comes up for you:

1. What beliefs were you raised with? What did you learn in school? What media images do you remember?

2. What were your actual interactions growing up?

3. What are your interactions/relationships today?

4. What roles do you see people of this race in? Boss, bus-driver, shop-keeper, co-worker, lover, etc.

5. What media images do you see today? Books, movies, newspapers, advertisements, TV, etc.

Journaling on these questions is only one part of the work. It's not enough to examine the stereotypes we carry about people different from ourselves—we want to replace them with truthful, fully realized stories and images. Reading is one way to begin building up memories of voices to challenge the stereotypes we have absorbed throughout our lives. Throughout the remainder of the workshop—and possibly beyond—try to add more voices by doing the following:

1. If you choose to watch a video, watch videos by or about people of color or about white people struggling with racism. Choose from the list in the Resources section or another video you have heard of that's not on the list.

2. White students, at least once a week, go some place where you are in the minority. For example, as a European-American, I could go to Lola's, a food market in the Mexican part of town, to buy tortillas and green peppers, instead of buying them at my local market, which caters to an upper-middle class, mostly white, clientele.

*Asian-American and Asian Pacific Islander*

_____

_____

_____

_____

_____

_____

_____

_____

_____

_____

*African-American*

_____

_____

_____

_____

_____

_____

_____

_____

_____

*Arab-American*

_____

_____

_____

_____

_____

_____

_____

_____

_____

_____

_____

*Chicano, La Raza, Puerto Rican, Hispanic, Latino*

_____

_____

_____

_____

_____

_____

_____

_____

_____

_____

_____

*Mixed race*

_____

_____

_____

_____

_____

_____

_____

_____

_____

*Native-American, Aleut*

_____

_____

_____

_____

_____

_____

_____

_____

_____

_____

*White, European-American*

_____

_____

_____

_____

_____

_____

_____

_____

_____

*Jewish-American*

_____

_____

_____

_____

_____

_____

_____

_____

_____

## Exercises: Welcoming New Voices

Communication is a basic human activity, a necessary tool for interpersonal relationships, but one that requires skills that aren't always learned or valued. Because it is so basic to relationship, communication is an important dynamic to attend to in race relations.

Communication can be effective or ineffective just as it also has the power to increase pleasure or cause pain. Communication comes in many forms, but when spoken or written, requires the use of language. Language, having developed along with the society that uses it, reflects societal attitudes and thinking. As a result, our common terminology, symbols, and language structures may reinforce racism and white privilege. The first exercise will sensitize you to bias in the English language.

The next exercises address the personal interplay of communication. Spoken communication requires a listener and a speaker. Feeling unheard or misunderstood can be a frustrating and emotional experience, and can drive you to anger or tears, as can being accused of not listening when you think you are.

We may learn to avoid communication problems by restricting our interactions to those we are comfortable with. Unfortunately, we are often uncomfortable with people different from ourselves. By learning more about your own reactions when communication becomes difficult, you can begin to find ways to continue talking instead of shutting down or becoming angry. You will look at ways of beginning to welcome those voices you may have been excluding.

### Language

In common use of the English language we may unthinkingly per-petuate racist stereotypes. This exercise will help you understand how our own racial attitudes have been conditioned since child-hood by the power of words and help you begin to read and listen critically so as to interrupt that conditioning. Discuss your findings in a group or work together to answer the questions.

1. Look up the definitions for "black" and "white" in the dictionary. Compare their meanings.

2. Write down a list of expressions that use the words "black" or "white " (for example, "blackmail" or "white lie") and consider the meanings of those expressions.

3. There are often several ways to say the same thing and each way may have different impact. For example, consider the difference between describing urban poor as "economically disadvantaged" or "economically exploited." Or why do we refer to people of color as minorities when they actually comprise a majority of the world's people? Pick up a mainstream magazine and read through it, seeing how many examples you can find where words used to describe people of color imply that they are less than.

4. Loaded words are those that carry cultural meaning. They may seem fine in one context but carry historical baggage when used in another. For example, in battles between Native Americans and whites for control of North America, Indian victories are often described as massacres while U.S. government victories are described as victories. What other loaded words are often used in describing Native Americans that cause us to forget that they are human beings with complex, highly refined, cultures (for example, "savage," "squaw"). What loaded words are used in describing peo-ple in developing nations (for example, "huts" used to describe vil-lage houses)? Keeping the concept of loaded words in mind, see how many examples you hear or read over the coming week.

5. Sometimes qualifying adjectives used in describing a person are used in a racist manner. For example, in an article on police/civilian relations, a spokesperson for a Chicano neighborhood association is described as "an intelligent young man" while the police represen-tative is simply introduced as "the Task Force chair." Why do we

need to be told that the Chicano is intelligent? Return to your magazine and look for examples where adjectives such as "qualified," "well-dressed," "intelligent," and so forth are used in a racist way.

6. Passive tense can easily be used to hide agency. For example, we read that "slaves were brought to America." Who brought those enslaved African people to America? Or another book states that "the continental railroad was built," leaving out information about the Chinese workers who built much of it. Look through some books or magazines for similar examples of using the passive voice.

### Hearing and Being Heard

"Voices" is about seeking to broaden your experiences, listen with different ears, explore hearing and being heard in the largest sense. After quietly reflecting on the questions listed below, make notes of your thoughts and feelings on each. Then share your responses with a partner.

*Notes* _____

When have you felt unheard?

_____

_____

_____

_____

What don't you like to hear?

_____

_____

_____

_____

How do you keep from hearing what you don't like to hear?

_____

_____

_____

_____

### *Where Are the Voices of People of Color*

Think of the voices you hear regularly throughout your day (for example, morning radio, workplace, family gatherings, entertainment). Who is speaking? What do they look like? Do they have authority? Are they entertaining? After you've completed the picture of whose voices you hear, answer the following questions:

- If you don't currently hear many voices of people of color, what changes can you make in your life to ensure you will?

- What can you do to help ensure that the voices of people of color are heard (for example, in friendship groups, the workplace, community meetings, and so on)?

*Notes* _____

_____

_____

_____

_____

_____

_____

_____

_____

_____

_____

_____

_____

_____

# Section IV

## *FEAR*

## Overcoming the Barrier of Fear

This section examines fear from three different perspectives:

- The fear white people are conditioned to have of people of color

- The fear people of color have of white people based on personal and historical events

- The fear we all have of confronting and talking about racism and white privilege

For white people, fear of people of color, in particular African-American men, emerges in many unconscious acts. For example, they may automatically lock car doors when entering certain neighborhoods or clutch a purse close when young men of color pass on the sidewalk. Whites may offer specific incidents in their life to explain such fears, but there is much more at work in shaping white fear than personal incidents. In readings and group exercises, you will examine ways in which family messages, cultural influences, and the media condition white people to fear people of color.

Several readings explore how fear of white violence shapes the lives of people of color. A brief look at history reveals the numerous ways in which white people have systematically terrorized people of color in this country.

As a means of identifying your own personal fears, you will gather your courage to name the fears that arise in cross-racial interactions. White people, in particular, also need to specify what they fear will happen if they call attention to perceived racism or try to make white privilege visible. With your fears clearly visible, you will look at what it takes to move through them so that you can begin to see the world for yourself, instead of through the blinding lens of fear.

## Readings: The Cycle of Fear

These readings examine the fears people of color have of white people, how white people are conditioned to fear people of color, and the fears that arise for anyone confronting racism and white privilege.

- bell hooks looks at the fear African-Americans have of white people in an excerpt from "Whiteness in the Black Imagination"

- In "Believing in Ourselves," Carla Trujillo discusses the importance of examining and talking about our fears.

- An excerpt from *By the Color of Our Skin* by Leonard Steinhorn and Barbara Diggs-Brown analyzes a pervasive image in the media today—the black man as a violent or criminal outlaw.

- Joy Harjo's poem, "Give You Back," asks for release from fear so she can live life fully.

### Whiteness in the Black Imagination (excerpt)

*In the following excerpt from "Whiteness in the Black Imagination," bell hooks discusses the fear that black folk may associate with whiteness, examining histori-cal and present-day causes.* From bell hooks, "Whiteness in the Black Imagi-nation" in *Killing Rage: Ending Racism* 1995, p. 39. Copyright (c) 1995 Henry Holt and Company. Source: Henry Holt and Company.

Looking past stereotypes to consider various representations of whiteness in the black imagination, I appeal to memory, to my earli-est recollections of ways these issues were raised in black life. Returning to memories of growing up in the social circumstances created by racial apartheid, to all black spaces on the edges of town, I reinhabit a location where black folks associated whiteness with the terrible, the terrifying, the terrorizing. White people were regarded as terrorists, especially those who dared to enter that seg-regated space of blackness. As a child, I did not know any white people. They were strangers, rarely seen in our neighborhoods. The "official" white men who came across the tracks were there to sell products, Bibles, and insurance. They terrorized by economic exploitation. What did I see in the gazes of those white men who crossed our thresholds that made me afraid, that made black chil-dren unable to speak? Did they understand at all how strange their whiteness appeared in our living rooms, how threatening? Did they journey across the tracks with the same "adventurous" spirit that other white men carried to Africa, Asia, to those mysterious places they would one day call the "third world"? Did they come to our houses to meet the Other face-to-face and enact the colonizer role, dominating us on our own turf ?

Their presence terrified me. Whatever their mission, they looked too much like the unofficial white men who came to enact rituals of ter-ror and torture. As a child, I did not know how to tell them apart, how to ask the "real white people to please stand up." The terror that I felt is one black people have shared. Whites learn about it sec-ondhand. Confessing in *Soul Sister* that she too began to feel this ter-ror after changing her skin to appear "black" and going to live in the South, Grace Halsell described her altered sense of whiteness:

> Caught in this climate of hate, I am totally terror-stricken, and I search my mind to know why I am fearful of my own people. Yet they no longer seem my people, but rather the "enemy" arrayed in large numbers against me in some hostile territory.... My wild heartbeat is a secondhand kind of terror. I know that I cannot possibly experience what *they*, the black people, experience....

Black folks raised in the North do not escape this sense of terror. In her autobiography, *Every Good-bye Ain't Gone*, Itabari Njeri begins the narrative of her northern childhood with a memory of southern roots. Traveling south as an adult to investigate the murder of her grandfather by white youth who were drag racing and ran him down in the streets, Njeri recalls that for many years "the distant and accidental violence that took my grandfather's life could not compete with the psychological terror that had begun to engulf my own." Ultimately, she begins to link that terror with the history of black people in the United States, seeing it as an imprint carried from the past to the present:

> As I grew older, my grandfather assumed mythic proportions in my imagination. Even in absence, he filled my room like music and watched over me when I was fearful. His fantasized presence diverted thoughts of my father's drunken rages. With age, my fantasizing ceased, the image of my grandfather faded. What lingered was the memory of his caress, the pain of something missing in my life, wrenched away by reckless white youths. I had a growing sense—the beginning of an inevitable comprehension—that this society deals blacks a disproportionate share of pain and denial.

### Believing in Ourselves

*In this essay, Carla Trujillo talks about how fear of doing it wrong often prevents us from taking the steps necessary to bridge our differences. Although addressed to women, this is equally applicable to men.* From Carla Trujillo, "Believing in Ourselves" in *Skin Deep: Women Writing on Color, Culture, and Identity,* edited by Elena Featherston, 1994, p. 181. Copyright (c) 1994 Crossing Press. Source: Crossing Press.

The common boundary of "woman," per se, is often not enough to compensate for other areas of difference, particularly along the lines of race, class, and sexual preference. Each and every one of us is affected in some way by society's unjust views. Creating community means we must all make a continual effort to rid these poisons from our hearts and minds. Similarly, we must seek to dispel our insecurities about feeling that we need to be perfect with respect to the issues of racism, sexism, homophobia, and so on. Fear of making errors keeps us defensive, hostile, and unable to truly open up to one another.

I have accepted the fact that I am not a perfect person, but I am committed to unlearning old behaviors, prejudices, and unhealthy coping mechanisms. This process brings up a lot of fear that, I am sure, many of us can relate to. Recognizing our fears and talking about them to someone who cares about us enables us to work through them. This is growth and it's never easy.

I have also found that if I am vulnerable to others, they in turn are often vulnerable to me. Folks open up, listen, and learn. This can be scary, but I find that I have opened up my heart and the hearts of many others to positive growth.

When I am at my lowest ebb and filled with despair over our treatment of the world and one another, someone will surprise me and tell me that she is volunteering at a shelter for homeless teenagers, learning Spanish, or simply sitting with someone who is dying of cancer. When this happens, I sit for a minute and remember that we can still believe in ourselves and in our capacity for retaining our humanity. This, for me, is the ultimate in creating community.

### By the Color of Our Skin (excerpt)

By the Color of Our Skin, *written by a white man and a black woman, takes a cold hard look at the rhetoric and reality of integration in the U.S. In the excerpt presented here, the authors show the truth behind the pervasive image of the violent black man and describe how that image contributes to the fear white people have of black men.* From Leonard Steinhorn and Barbara Diggs-Brown, *By the Color of Our Skin: The Illusion of Integration and the Reality of Race*, 1999, pp. 171-173. Copyright (c) Dutton Press, an imprint of Penguin Putnam Inc. Source: Dutton Press.

The anger-entitlement image tells whites that blacks can make it in America only through illegitimate means. So too does the other image that took hold during the 1960s, an image that remains an insidious influence today: the black man as a violent or criminal outlaw. What makes this image so strong and resilient are its many sources in culture and society. It is part romance, part fear. It is part exploitation, part self-destruction. It is part pose, part reality. It gathers momentum in the news media, in the entertainment media, in urban street culture, and in more than three hundred years of black-white dynamics. It is driven by the imagination of white conservatives, white liberals, black and white academics, and Hollywood moguls. Law-and-order politicians have built careers exploiting this image much the way radical intellectuals have gained fame celebrating it. It is also an image in which whites see themselves as victims. The fact that most black Americans are sickened by crime in their neighborhoods and want the criminals locked away does not seem to soften this image. Nor does the fact that only a tiny proportion of blacks actually commit violent crimes—only about a tenth of one percent of blacks fifteen to thirty-four years old are charged with homicide each year.[1] Nor the fact that white Americans themselves have high rates of violent crimes: the U.S. murder rate without counting black homicides would still far surpass that of Europe and Britain.[2] The image of blacks as primitive that made antebellum whites in the South fear for their daughters has ripened into the one of threatening, uncontrollable, alienated blacks who have robbed our lives and neighborhoods of their pristine innocence.

Whatever the mitigating facts or factors, no one should deny the troubling reality of crime, particularly black-on-black crime, in parts of urban America. Because of this reality we are able to wrap the image of the black as an outlaw in the clinical language of crime statistics and law enforcement jargon. But underneath the numbers is a caricature that taints almost every black man. By a subliminal logic, white fear of the underclass becomes fear of the violent criminal, fear of urban America, and, finally, fear of all black men. Civil rights groups rightly criticized the *Los Angeles Times* for a 1981 article headlined MARAUDERS FROM INNER CITY PREY ON L.A.'S SUBURBS, but the headline was merely a manifestation of a deep and abiding dread. White fear of black violence is almost a reflexive response, regardless of contrary evidence or experience. A 1989 *Nightline* broadcast showed this graphically when white pedestrians recoiled with visceral fear and uncertainty when black high school students asked them for change for a dollar, even though the black teens were neatly dressed and the street was full of people.[3] In Oak Park, Illinois, long considered a model integrated community, all the years of living together and building trust did not diminish the reflex among whites after a couple of 1994 incidents involving black and white teens. "When my kids are beaten up and bloody, and it's black kids causing the problem, what am I supposed to think?" one white mother asked.[4]

The image is so ingrained, so pervasive that individual illustrations barely do it justice. It is woven so finely into daily life that most white Americans barely blink when hearing that jewelry store owners bar young black men from their stores, that black college students are questioned about a crime near campus, or that whites steer clear of large black gatherings, as they do in Atlanta, when whites avoid downtown during the annual Freaknik party for black college students, or as they did in Washington, D.C., the day of the Million Man March. It is an image so powerful that some advertising executives say there's no point in featuring a black man in an ad about a luxury car because whites will end up associating the car with drug dealers or crime.[5]

The outlaw image has become a filter through which whites imagine, see, and think about black men. When a promising black Bay Area basketball player didn't score the minimum on his college entrance exams, he was written off in the media as yet another inner-city kid lost to a culture of crack, alienation, and crime—until a black *Oakland Tribune* columnist probed further and found the youngster studying hard, improving his grades, and serving as the sole supporter of his mother and sister.[6] When Donald Cherry, a white man, told Nashville police that his toddler had been shot to death by some black teens after a traffic dispute, everyone believed him—just as they did Charles Stuart and Susan Smith—until his story began to unravel and Cherry finally admitted that he was trying to buy drugs when his child was killed.[7] When black students at an elite private high school near Washington, D.C., wanted to hold a go-go dance, school administrators balked, certain it would lead to violence, until one of the black teachers reassured them and the dance took place without incident.[8] "The image is that young black men are like dry tinder waiting for an idle spark to set them off," observed Harvard professor Henry Louis Gates, Jr.[9] To most whites a white teenager in sweatpants is a jock, but a black teen in sweats is trouble. When a 1989 *ABC/Washington Post* poll asked whether it was "common sense" or "prejudice" for whites to avoid black neighborhoods because of crime, three-quarters answered common sense.[10] "My appearance is not menacing, but I am perceived to be a menace," wrote a Harvard-educated black man in a letter to the *New York Times.* "It is unfortunate but true that every black male is Willie Horton and Willie Horton is every black male."[11]

1. Richard Harwood, "America's Unchecked Epidemic," *Washington Post*, December 1, 1997, p. A25.

2. Franklin E. Zimring and Gordon Hawkins, *Crime Is Not the Problem: Lethal Violence in America* (New York: Oxford University Press, 1997), p. 81.

3. The *Nightline* broadcast was aired April 27, 1989.

4. Sharon Cotliar, "Oak Park Struggling to Get Along," *Chicago Sun-Times*, July 24, 1994, p. A48.

5. On the advertising executives, see Marilyn Kern-Foxworth, *Aunt Jemima, Uncle Ben, and Rastus* (Westport, Conn.: Greenwood Press, 1994), P. 159.

6. Howard Bryant, "The Search for Role Models," in Thinking Black, ed. by DeWayne Wickam (New York: Crown, 1997), pp. 81-85.

7. "Tenn. Man Admits Fabricating Tale of Traffic Dispute in Son's Death," *Washington Post*, October 24, 1996, p. A7.

8. For the private school story see Patricia Elam Ruff, "Private School, Private Pain," Washington Post, February 23, 1997. pp. C1-2.

9. Interview with Henry Louis Gates, Jr., "A 'Race Man' Argues For a Broader Curriculum," *Time*, April 22, 1991, p. 16.

10. Michel McQueen, "People with the Least to Fear From Crime Drive the Crime Issue," Wall Street Journal, August 12, 1992, p. A1.

11. Donald L. Chatman, "Willie Horton and Me," letter to the editor, New York Times, September 24, 1989, section 6, p. 12.

*FEAR*

## I Give You Back

*Joy Harjo's poem "I Give You Back" powerfully illustrates the origin of fears she carries as a member of the Creek tribe and the benefits of releasing those fears.* From Joy Harjo, "I Give You Back" from *She Had Some Horses*, 1983, Copyright (c) 1983 Thunder's Mouth Press. Source: Thunder's Mouth Press/ Avalon Publishing Group.

I release you, my beautiful and terrible
fear. I release you. You were my beloved
and hated twin, but now, I don't know you
as myself. I release you with all the
pain I would know at the death of
my daughters.

You are not my blood anymore.

I give you back to the white soldiers
who burned down my home, beheaded my children,
raped and sodomized my brothers and sisters.
I give you back to those who stole the
food from our plates when we were starving.

I release you, fear, because you hold
these scenes in front of me and I was born
with eyes that can never close.

I release you, fear, so you can no longer
keep me naked and frozen in the winter,
or smothered under blankets in the summer.

I release you
I release you
I release you
I release you


I am not afraid to be angry.
I am not afraid to rejoice.
I am not afraid to be black.
I am not afraid to be white.
I am not afraid to be hungry.
I am not afraid to be full.
I am not afraid to be hated.
I am not afraid to be loved.

to be loved, to be loved, fear.

Oh, you have choked me, but I gave you the leash.
You have gutted me but I gave you the knife.
You have devoured me, but I laid myself across the fire.
You held my mother down and raped her,
                    but I gave you the heated thing.

I take myself back, fear.
You are not my shadow any longer.
I won't hold you in my hands.
You can't live in my eyes, my ears, my voice
my belly, or in my heart my heart
my heart     my heart

But come here, fear
I am alive and you are so afraid
                              of dying.

## Reflecting: Creating Fear

The media often presents words and images that make white people fearful of people of color. Movies, TV shows, advertisements, newspapers, magazines, and radio all contribute to such misconceptions as young African-American men are all gang members.

For example, in San Francisco on a main street through a largely Chicano/Latino neighborhood, a billboard portrays an elegant white woman sitting in her car. The ad is for a cell phone to call for help. The implication is that the neighborhood is too dangerous to get out of the car and use a pay phone or that no one in the neighborhood could be trusted to help.

Write down other examples of how the media teaches white people to fear people of color.

*Notes* _____

_____

_____

_____

_____

_____

_____

_____

_____

_____

_____

_____

_____

## Exercises: Confronting Our Fears

Bringing out your own fears to examine and comparing them with the fears of others can help you understand that your fears are not unique. We all hold numerous fears associated with interracial interactions, talking about race, and examining white privilege and racism. In the exercises you name your own fears, listen to others name their fears, and strategize together ways to overcome them.

### Naming Fears

In groups divided into white and people of color, discuss the following questions and make an extensive list of fears. After, come together and compare the differences and similarities between the answers of white people and people of color. If you are not working in a multiracial setting, try to answer for those not represented based on the readings or your knowledge of history.

1. What do you fear in cross-racial interactions? For example, you may fear saying something insensitive. For people of color, specifically what do you fear in interactions with white people? For example, you may feel being ignored.

2. What do you feel in calling attention to white privilege and racism? For example, you may fear that you've misanalyzed the situation in pointing out racism in action.

*Notes* _____

_____

_____

_____

_____

_____

_____

_____

_____

_____

_____

_____

_____

### Thinking about the Readings

Find a partner and with your partner, discuss the following questions. Think back to the readings as you talk about the issues. Take notes to share with the group.

1. Does fear of making errors keep you defensive, hostile, and unable to open up to other people?

_____

_____

_____

_____

_____

2. What are some fears people of color have developed in response to their own experience and that of their ancestors in regard to interactions with white people or calling attention to racism and white privilege?

_____

_____

_____

_____

_____

3. How do the fears white people have of calling attention to racism and white privilege differ from those of people of color?

_____

_____

_____

_____

_____

### Strategies for Transcending Fear

What are some strategies for moving through fear, acting in spite of the fear? For example, be willing to make a mistake. List all the ways you can think of to work with fear so it doesn't block you.

*Notes* _____

_____

_____

_____

_____

_____

_____

_____

_____

_____

_____

_____

_____

_____

_____

_____

_____

_____

_____

_____

*FEAR*

# Section V

## *GUILT and SHAME*

## Acknowledging Guilt and Shame

Feelings of guilt and shame are common reactions for white people who begin to examine their own white privilege and learn how it is based on an ongoing history of oppression of people of color. For example, white people may carry guilt about the history of slavery, the genocide of native American Indians, and the internment of Japanese-Americans during World War II. Anyone learning about history or current events through the eyes of the conquered and oppressed, may ask, "How could I not know this?" and then feel guilty and ashamed of their ignorance and unconscious participation.

*Guilt* is defined as the discomfort you feel when you have done something to harm another person or violate a moral prohibition. Guilt tells you that you have done something wrong and need to do something about it. When you are personally responsible for a wrong doing, guilt is an appropriate and healthy response that can lead us to a healing action that corrects the wrong. But guilt may become irrational, making you feel responsible for what you have no control over.

A common example of irrational guilt in white people is to think that because of white privilege, they are always in the wrong in interracial conflict. They then romanticize people of color, seeing them as always in the right. Creating such generalizations feeds white self-hatred, glorifies and sentimentalizes people of color, and does nothing to build a world where all people are treated equally as individuals. In this section you will learn to distinguish between useful, rational guilt and irrational, immobilizing guilt. You'll look at how to resist romanticization, with its tendency toward stereotypes and dual thinking. Then, when guilt alerts you to harmful behavior, you will be ready to figure out how to remedy the harm. Unlike the temporary fix of comforting words or forgiveness from the injured party, making reparation can truly free you of guilt.

*Shame* is defined as what you feel when you fail to live up to your own ideals. In its extreme, shame can make you feel exposed as a bad person and see yourself as helpless to change. Sometimes feelings of shame can turn to anger with the person who caused you to feel ashamed, an important area of concern for white people in interactions with people of color. In personal and group exercises, you'll examine shameful incidents in your past in an effort to reduce your burden of shame and learn how to use shame productively.

When guilt and shame keep us from having real authentic relationships, we maintain our stereotypes, our fears, and our ignorance. We need to know each other as the unique human beings we are, not just as a member of a racial/ethnic group. We need to study an inclusive history and increase our understanding of the forces that have shaped our lives, but not with the goal of finding someone to blame. We need to be able to tell the truth to each other, to experience the normal conflicts of personality differences, and to express appropriate anger free from the baggage of unconscious racist messages.

Confronting your guilt and shame can help you feel positive about yourself. Instead of reacting blindly to uncomfortable feelings, you increase your ability to think independently and to stand up against oppression in its many forms. You can then take full responsibility for your actions, own up to your mistakes, learn from them, and go forward.

## Readings: Focusing on Guilt and Shame

The readings in this section range from analytical and theoretical to deeply personal. They describe and distinguish guilt and shame, challenging you to confront guilt and learn how to manage it.

- In "Rethinking the Role of Guilt and Shame in White Women's Antiracism Work" Clare Holzman defines guilt and shame, helping you see how they can both help and hurt white people who are engaged in confronting white privilege.

- You may need to look for and acknowledge shameful actions of your ancestors, as does Aurora Levins Morales in "Raícism."

- "Breaking Old Patterns, Weaving New Ties" by Margo Adair and Sharon Howell describes how white guilt can lead to self-hatred and romanticizing the oppressed.

- In "Integrating a Burning House," Harry Belafonte and Cornel West reflect on the unrealized dream of the civil rights movement—that we would have the moral power and the force not only to change the political landscape but to change the moral landscape of this country as well. What is our responsibility in this?

## Rethinking the Role of Guilt and Shame in White Women's Anti-racism Work

*Although this article was written as a guide for therapists working with white women and has a narrow focus, we find it to be one of the best descriptions of guilt and shame in general and how these impact white people who are engaged in anti-racism work.* From Clare Holzman, "Rethinking the Role of Guilt and Shame in White Women's Antiracism Work" in *Racism in the Lives of Women: Testimony, Theory, and Guides to Antiracist Practice,* edited by Jeanne Adleman, MA, and Gloria Enguîdanos, Ph.D., 1995, pp. 75-77. Copyright (c) 1995 The Haworth Press. Source: The Haworth Press.

In antiracism workshops I have taken part in and in my reading about antiracism training, the subject of guilt keeps coming up (Katz, 1978, p. 137; Landerman and McAtee, 1982, p. 24; Northwestern University Women's Center Campus Climate Project, 1989; Pheterson, 1986, p. 152; Pinderhughes, 1989, pp. 99-100). There is widespread agreement that guilt is an immediate, powerful response of white women learning about racism, and I seem to be no exception. There is almost equally widespread agreement that my guilt is unproductive and that I should cut it out; but for some reason I continue to feel guilty. This paper is the result of my efforts to understand what is going on inside me that I have been calling guilt, and how I can learn to work through it so that it will be less of an obstacle to my progress toward antiracism.

I have come to three conclusions. First, not all guilt is unproductive. In moderate doses, guilt motivates me to keep trying to change. Second, much of what others and I have been calling guilt may often be shame, which can also be productive if it isn't excessive. Third, when I am trying to explore and modify my racism, whether in an antiracism training situation or in therapy, I am the most open to learning when I am treated in a way that does not itself generate irrational and overwhelming guilt and shame. Furthermore, there are times when what is most useful to me is help in formulating concepts and strategies for coping with my guilt and shame instead of being immobilized by them. If the needs of the group call for a different kind of process, it is my responsibility to seek out other opportunities to work through my guilt and shame issues.

Guilt and shame have been defined in many contradictory ways (Ausubel, 1955; Banman, 1988; Kaufman, 1985; Klein, 1975a, Lewis, 1971). The following definitions are my composite of the ideas that I have found most helpful in my own self-exploration:

Guilt is the discomfort I feel when I have done something that harms another person or violates a moral prohibition. Guilt, like anxiety, is a signal that something is amiss and needs to be corrected. Anxiety tells me that I am in danger and need to make myself safer. Guilt tells me that I have done something wrong and need to correct it or make reparation. Irrational guilt is either guilt over something I am not actually responsible for, or guilt whose intensity is disproportionate to the offense.

Shame is what I feel when I fail to live up to my ideals for myself. Shame, like guilt, is a signal that prompts me to change my behavior. The focus is not on the harm done to others, but on the defect in myself. Shame involves feelings of exposure and an impulse to hide. In fact, the Indo-European root of the word "shame" also means "to hide. " Irrational shame is a feeling of having been exposed as a fundamentally and irremediably defective human being.

As a white woman living in a racially oppressive society, I have much to feel realistically guilty about. I benefit daily from racial oppression without even having to be aware of it (McIntosh, 1988). To the extent that I passively accept the fruits of my white privilege, I am guilty of colluding with racism to harm its targets for my own benefit. Furthermore, because I have internalized the racist attitudes and beliefs of my society, I often speak and act in racist ways that directly or indirectly harm people of color. When I become aware of a specific way in which I have been passively or actively racist, I feel guilty. This guilt is constructive to the extent that it motivates me to change my attitudes and behavior and to work toward changing racist institutions. I can never be free of this guilt until I live in a society that is no longer racist and until I have overcome my own racism.

My guilt is unproductive when it is misdirected, or when it is so intense that it immobilizes me instead of motivating me. One way this can happen is that my rational guilt can trigger irrational guilt based on early childhood fantasies (Klein, 1975a) or on actual childhood experiences. Another is that I may fail to make a clear distinction between what I am personally responsible for and what I have no control over. Thus, I am responsible for my own actions or failures to act, but I am not responsible for the actions of my ancestors or for the existence of the entire structure of institutionalized racism. Preoccupation with guilt over things beyond my control is often an avoidance of facing the things I can control; making reparation often involves giving something up or doing something difficult or frightening.

The remedy for excessive guilt is to clarify what is real and what is fantasy, what is my responsibility and what is not, and then to turn my attention to what I can do about it in the real world. According to Klein, one of the fringe benefits of making reparation at a reality level is that it reduces the intensity of unconscious guilt as well, freeing me for greater creativity and productive work (1975, pp. 335-336).

I will have difficulty moving past guilt to constructive work if I am using my guilt to persuade myself that I am a good person (Lewis, p. 44), or to elicit sympathy, or to ward off anticipated attack by others. All of these shift the focus from examining racism to taking care of me. They are especially damaging in group settings where there are women of color present and I turn to them to comfort me and relieve me of my guilt by forgiving me (Pheterson, 1986; Root, 1989). Although comforting words and expressions of forgiveness may be temporarily soothing, the only lasting way to be free of rational guilt is to make reparation.

I said earlier that much of what gets labeled as guilt in antiracism work is in fact shame. Guilt and shame often occur together or sequentially, so it is easy to confuse them (Banman, 1988, p. 85; Lewis, 1971, pp. 27-28). When I feel guilty, I am focused on the harm I have done to the other person or the rule I have broken, and I want to make reparation. When I feel ashamed, I am focused on feelings of exposure, acute self-consciousness, and worthlessness, and I want to hide. Guilt can induce shame, because I may believe that my transgression was caused by my deficiency and reveals it to others. Banman describes a shame/guilt cycle in which "the humiliated fury often experienced in shame leads to an aggressive fantasy or impulse. This impulse usually triggers guilt and inhibition, but since inhibition is perceived as passivity and failure, shame follows" (p. 85). Guilt can also be a defense against shame, and vice versa (Banman, 1988, p. 85; Lewis, 1971, p. 27).

Because I hold the ideal of being nonracist, I will experience shame whenever I am confronted with the persistence of my racism. Since I have been raised in a shame-bound family within a shame-bound culture, healthy shame quickly triggers irrational shame in me. For the moment, I feel that I have exposed myself as a hopeless case, someone who is inherently racist and always will be, or someone who is too stupid, selfish, lazy, or heartless to do the work required to overcome it. At that moment I feel numb and paralyzed. The reactivation of developmentally early shaming experiences throws me back to a time when I had few resources to draw on in coping with my shame (Alonso and Rutan, 1988). I feel helpless, impotent, and vulnerable. When I feel intense shame, I am unable to think clearly or act effectively. I just want the ground to open and swallow me up. Obviously this is not a productive emotional state in which to try to learn what to do about racism.

Becoming aware that I am feeling shame, especially if I am being observed by others, is itself a shaming experience (Kaufman, 1985, p. 29; Lewis, 1971, p. 27). I feel that if I am experiencing shame, I must have something to be ashamed of, and now everyone else will know it too. For this reason, and because shame has its origins in preverbal experiences, I rarely talk about my shame, so I have few opportunities to resolve it (Alonso and Rutan, 1988, p. 6). Instead, I carry within me an enormous reservoir of old shame that is waiting to be reactivated by any new shaming experience.

One way in which I can prepare myself to confront my racism is to arrange for supportive environments in which to work through old shame so that the total burden that is waiting to sandbag me will be reduced. Then when I work on unlearning my racism I can give myself permission to experience rational shame without fearing that it will trigger a catastrophic reaction.

When I feel either guilt or shame, I often become angry with the person I perceive as the cause of my distressing feelings (Banman, 1988, p. 85;). I also project my own "badness" onto the other person (Klein, 1975). Both of these mechanisms prompt me to attack the other person by counterblaming (Zuk and Zuk, 1987, p. 224). This diverts attention from my faults to those of someone else. It allows me to feel powerful instead of helpless, and creates distance between me and the other person so that I feel less vulnerable. In order to identify and work on my racism. I must learn to recognize and restrain my impulse to counterblame and keep the focus on examining myself.

Guilt and shame are appropriate emotional responses to becoming aware of one's racism, and can be major sources of motivation for change. However, in order for these emotions to be productive rather than immobilizing, many white women will need a training or therapy experience that provides a structure, a conceptual framework, and concrete strategies for dealing with guilt and shame constructively and keeping them at or returning them to the rational level. In antiracism training settings, this experience may be one component of a larger program, or may be offered as a specialized workshop focusing on this particular topic. In therapy, it will be helpful for the therapist to keep in mind that whenever the issue of racism comes up, whether it is raised by the client as something she wants to work on or by the therapist in response to racism expressed by the client, issues of guilt and shame are likely to be present.

In order for a woman to risk the extreme vulnerability associated with guilt and shame, it is important that the trainer or therapist be scrupulously and explicitly respectful of her boundaries, dignity, and fundamental worth. Shaming techniques such as belittling, sarcasm, or expressions of disgust, contempt, or condemnation are counterproductive. They reproduce childhood shaming experiences and are likely to trigger irrational shame (Kaufman, 1985, pp. 18-22). In a group setting, the trainers must not only maintain these standards themselves, they also have the task of guiding the participants in maintaining them in relation to one another. For many white women, an important step in unlearning racism has been an attempt to become aware of all the racist ideas we have been harboring and suppressing and to express them out loud in order to get help in exploring them thoroughly (Adams and Schlesinger, 1988, pp. 208-210; Pinderhughes, 1989, pp. 224-225). This is a process that is never completed, and it is difficult for it to happen at all unless there is some assurance of safety from attack. In the absence of such safety, there is a tendency to parrot what is believed to be acceptable to the group, and for the learning process to be drastically inhibited. (Careful thought must be given to the impact of this process on any women of color who may be present. They should have the option of absenting themselves from the training at this point.)

An analysis of racism as a system that is imposed on individuals, both oppressors and oppressed, helps to alleviate irrational guilt and shame. The analysis developed by Ricky Sherover-Marcuse is a good example of this. It stresses that no one is born a racist or chooses to become a racist, that we all resisted and were damaged by our induction into the system, and that what we have learned can be unlearned.

A discussion of the normality, inevitability, and usefulness of guilt and shame in the process of unlearning racism will help a woman not to feel guilty and ashamed about feeling guilty and ashamed. She will benefit from encouragement to talk about these feelings when they arise, help in distinguishing rational from irrational. guilt or shame, and support in exploring how to move from feelings to constructive action.

People differ in the extent to which guilt and shame are central to their experience, and in their readiness to explore them. It is counterproductive to try to impose these concepts on a woman who does not perceive them as relevant to herself. In group settings, different women will be at different points in their resolution of guilt and shame issues, and the needs and goals of the group as a whole may call for a different focus. It is important, however, that these issues not be dismissed without providing some validation that they are legitimate causes for concern and that they can be worked through successfully.

To summarize, guilt and shame are powerful emotions that are frequently evoked when white women attempt to explore and modify their racism. Although intense, irrational guilt and shame can be immobilizing, moderate levels of these emotions can serve as useful signals that a woman is not living up to her standards for herself and as productive motivators for change. Therapists and trainers can help a woman to work through guilt and shame issues by providing a supportive environment in which to explore them, a conceptual framework for understanding them, and strategies for coping with them. The payoff is increased freedom to think clearly and act effectively in resisting racism.

1. The concept of race and the racial categories used are inventions of the human mind and have political consequences. There are valid objections to all of the terms currently in use to designate race, and yet we have to use some set of terms in order to communicate. In this paper "white women" means women who benefit from the privilege accorded to those who are so designated; "women of color" means women who experience racist oppression.

2. Katz (1978), Landerman and McAtee (1982), and Pinderhughes (1989) discuss the need to work through guilt feelings in the group. Although Landerman and McAtee describe guilt as a natural and inevitable part of the process for white women confronting racism, I have found no reference that considers it constructive. Katz talks about the need to transform guilt into a motivating force, and supports feelings of internal conflict and responsibility, but characterizes guilt per se as "self-indulgence" that "benefits no one." This concept may be specific to contemporary Anglo-American culture, with its emphasis on individualism. In some cultures, guilt and shame because of the actions of one's ancestors, family members, or others with whom one is closely connected may be an integral part of the culture. These cultures may also have institutionalized ways of coping with guilt and shame based on the behavior of others. I am grateful to Gloria Enguîdanos for bringing this to my attention.

### Raícism: Rootedness as Spiritual and Political Practice

*Understanding and acknowledging our part and the part of our ancestors in perpetuating racism can help free us from immobilizing guilt. In "Raícism" Aurora Levins Morales confronts the fact that her ancestors owned slaves.* From Aurora Levins Morales, "Racism: Rootedness as Spiritual and Political Practice" in *Medicine Stories: History, Culture, and the Politics of Integrity*, 1998, pp. 75-77. Copyright (c) South End Press. Reprinted with permission of South End Press.

~1~

Raícism—from raíces or roots—is the practice of rooting ourselves in the real, concrete histories of our people: our families, our local communities, and our ethnic communities. It is radical genealogy, history made personal. It is a keeping of accounts. Its intent is to pierce the immense, mind-deadening denial that permeates daily life in the United States, that drowns our deepest grief and horror about the founding and ongoing atrocities of racism, class and patriarchy in an endless chatter about trivialities. Oppression buries the actual lives of real and contradictory people in the crude generalizations of bigotry and punishes us for not matching the caricature, refusing all evidence of who we actually are in defiance of its tidy categories. It is a blunt instrument, used for bashing, not only our dangerous complexities, but also the ancient and permanent fact of our involvement with each other.

Raícism, or rootedness, is the choice to bear witness to our specific, contradictory, historical identities in relationship to one another. The decision to examine exactly who our ancestors, all of them, have been—with each other and with everyone else. It is an accounting of the debts and assets we have inherited, and acknowledging the precise nature of that inheritance is an act of spiritual and political integrity.

~2~

I grew up on stories of my mother's barrio childhood in Spanish Harlem and the Bronx, of near starvation in the early years of the Depression, of my grandmother's single dress. It was not until I went to the small Puerto Rican town of Toa Alta and examined the parish registers that I discovered five generations of slave-holding ancestors among the petty landed gentry of northeast Puerto Rico. For generations a handful of families held political and economic power, married their children to each other and consolidated their wealth with the purchase of enslaved human beings. I remember the feelings, as this reality dawned on me, of shame, but also of excitement. Over the years I had found peasants, small farmers, revolutionaries in my family tree. This was the thing I had not wanted to find. If I could figure out how to face it and consciously carry it, how to transform shame and denial into wholeness, perhaps I could find a way out of the numbness of privilege, not only for myself, but for the people I worked with in classes and workshops who came asking to learn.

So that day I wrote down the name of each and every slave held by my ancestors that I could find recorded in the registers. I have used my own family history with slavery to break silence: to acknowledge publicly and repeatedly my family debt to their coerced labor, to expose and reject family mythology about our "kind" treatment of slaves as a step in challenging the generalized myth of kind slavery in Puerto Rico, and to make a decision that although none of these people had chosen me as a descendant, I owed them the respect one gives to ancestors because their labor had made it possible for my forebears to grow up and thrive. I have also made it my responsibility to make African people visible in every discussion of Puerto Rican history in which I participate.

Taking full responsibility for the legacy of relationships that our ancestors have left us is empowering and radical. Guilt and denial and the urgently defensive pull to avoid blame require immense amounts of energy and are profoundly immobilizing. Giving them up can be a great relief. Deciding that we are in fact accountable frees us to act. Acknowledging our ancestors' participation in the oppression of others (and this is ultimately true of everyone if you really dig) and deciding to balance the accounts on their behalf leads to greater integrity and less shame, less self-righteousness and more righteousness, humility and compassion and a sense of proportion.

At the same time, uncovering the credit side of the accounts, not the suffering but the solidarity, persistence, love, hard work, creativity and soul of our forebears is also an obligation we owe them. We are the ones responsible for carrying that forward into our own time and for calling on our kin to do likewise. For people committed to liberation to claim our descent from the perpetrators is a renewal of faith in human beings. If slavers, invaders, commuters of genocide, inquisitors can beget abolitionists, resistance fighters, healers, community builders, then anyone can transform an inheritance of privilege or of victimization into something more fertile than either.

One of the rewards of discovering exactly who our people have been—and how and with whom they have lived—is the possibility of unimagined kinship. My Jewish ancestors were settled in the Ukraine as a buffer against Turkish invasion, alongside German Mennonites brought in to teach the formerly landless Jews about farming. At a talk in Wichita, Kansas, I was able to thank their descendants and claim a relationship between us, as Eastern European Jew and German Christian, other than that of genocidal anti-Semitism.

Mapping the specificity of our ethnicity also reveals hidden relationships. European Americans in this country need to find out in relationship to whom they became white. The answers will be very different for the descendants of a Scot from Iowa, an Irishwoman from Alabama, a New York Pole, a Louisiana French-Spanish Creole, a Texan with roots in 17th-century England and 19th-century Austria and a Romanian Jew who settled in turn-of-the-century San Francisco. Questions about our place within the megastructures of racism become intimate and carry personality. It becomes possible to see the choices we make right now as extensions of those inherited ones, and to choose more courageously as a result.

### *Breaking Old Patterns, Weaving New Ties: Guilt*

Breaking Old Patterns, Weaving New Ties *is a handbook for anti-racist white activists. The section on guilt describes how guilt can be a normal first reaction to learning about injustice. However, unexamined, guilt can be very destructive. Learning more about how white people have resisted racism can help.* From Margo Adair and Sharon Howell, Breaking Old Patterns, Weaving New Ties pp. 11-12. Copyright (c) Tools for Change. Source: Tools for Change.

When those of us with privilege begin to look at what we take for granted and who pays the price, our first reaction is to feel guilty because we have been socialized to see things in individual terms. Guilt gives rise both to a self-hatred on the one hand, and to a romanticizing of the oppressed on the other. The oppressed are always right—"they can do no wrong"—and conversely, the privileged are always wrong and "can do no right." Thus the initial recognition of injustice often moves people from the place of denying the humanity of others to denying their own humanity.

Guilt creates an atmosphere in which people with a heritage of oppression are reluctant to reveal their experience. They do not want to have to deal with the defensiveness that invariably gets provoked. This perpetuates a state of ignorance among those with privilege, maintaining the narrow norm. In this atmosphere a politics based on principles, mutual respect, support and accountability is impossible.

Guilt and self-hatred are automatic reactions in people who have been stripped of any sense of connection to their heritage. To justify and protect privilege, categories are created for those who qualify for it and those who don't. So "white" has been made the great melting pot for people of European descent. People from distinct and separate cultures have all been poured into the pot, rising to the top of society through the process of having their heritage boiled away. All that is left to identify with is how far up one has risen. People are judged by what they own; their character and wisdom are deemed irrelevant. Loyalty to collective struggle, to principles, people, place and past have evaporated. Opportunism is rewarded while generosity is seen as sentimental. *White is solely an identity of privilege.* This is the "wonderbreading of America."

People have always resisted dehumanization. Of course, we are not taught this in our schools. Just as the monoculture has obliterated the struggles of people of color to maintain and advance their humanity, it has wiped out our memory of those of European descent who refused to "strike the deal"—to relinquish principles in exchange for upward mobility. The history of white radicalism has been marginalized and made invisible. Few people know of William Lloyd Garrison, Wendell Phillips, the Grimke sisters, or Lillian Smith. Fewer still know anything about those in the South who resisted secession.

So whites working in today's progressive movements are faced with feelings of isolation and illegitimacy. The heritage from which we can take pride is gone, replaced only with privileges which we know have been made possible through genocide and exploitation. The reduction of history to the victimization of the oppressed and the vilification of the privileged makes it impossible to draw upon the past as a source of pride, inspiration, and sustenance.

## Integrating a Burning House

*Harry Belafonte and Cornel West talk about the difficulty of retaining an ethical and moral vision while keeping it real. How do we live up to our own ideals while struggling to be successful in a country where white supremacy pervades every nook and cranny?* From Harry Belafonte and Cornel West, "Integrating a Burning House" in *Restoring Hope: Conversations on the Future of Black America* by Cornel West and Kelvin Shawn Sealey, 1997, pp. 24-26. Copyright © 1997 Beacon Press. Source: Beacon Press.

HB: The last thing Dr. King ever said to me he said standing in my home just before be went down to Memphis. We had strategized and put some things together. He seemed very agitated. And everybody had left the meeting. Andy Young was there, Bernard Lee, my wife, Dr. King, and myself. His shoes were off, and he was just walking up and down and muttering to himself, and I said, "What's the matter, Martin?" He said, "I don't know. I'm troubled." I said, "About what?" He said, "You know, we fought long and hard for integration, as we should have. And I know we're going to get it. That's a *fait accompli*. But I tell you, Harry, I've come on a realization that really deeply troubles me." I said, "Well, what is it?" He said, "I've come to the realization that I think we may be integrating into a burning house." And that really threw me. Because my fantasy was that we would have the moral power and the force not only to change the political landscape but to change the moral landscape of this country as well. And if you change the moral landscape, you can come to a compassionate place about the poor, the disenfranchised, the lame, the old, all the things that we crush in this country, all the things that we find disposable: poor people, black people, homeless people, old people, crippled people, mentally ill people, all those things we want to kill off. The new politics.

So I tell you, yes, I feel that we have lost an awful lot. And we have done it in the name of integration. This is the first time in the history of our people in this country where we have no leader outside the system. The only one who speaks outside the system is Farrakhan. He's captured the hearts and the imaginations of millions of young black people because he's outside the system. The rest of us are in the system. All those young civil rights leaders, all those great leaders—whether it's Jesse Jackson or John Lewis—we're all in the system. We're in the Congress, we're in the government, and we're playing their game. We have to be re-elected. We have to aspire to the presidency. We are the chiefs of the army. We have all these titles, but we've lost our humanity, we've lost our vision, we've lost our culture. And how do we get back to it? I do not see our leaders coming together some place and creating the new Du Bois, the new Robeson, the new Martin King, the new Fanny Lou Hamer, the new Ella Baker.

CW. And that raises this issue of hope, you know. The great Eugene O'Neill, you might recall, when he arrived here in 1946 to put on his play *The Iceman Cometh*, was asked to comment on America. He said, "It's the best example of a country that exemplifies the question, What does it profit a man or woman to gain the world and lose its soul?" And there's a sense in which fifty years later, artists like yourself and Coltrane and Toni Morrison and others are trying to say, as the young people do, how do we keep it real? That is to say, how can we be realistic about what this nation is about and still sustain hope, acknowledging that we're up against so much? When I talk to young people these days, there's a sense in which they're in an anti-idealist mode and mood. They want to keep it real. And keeping it real means, in fact, understanding that the white supremacy you thought you could push back permeates every nook and cranny of this nation so deeply that you ought to wake up and recognize how deep it is.

That to me is a very serious challenge. If we were to take them back to '65, and, say, put black faces in high places, and think that somehow the problem was going to be solved, they'd say to us, Don't you realize how naive that is? And they don't say that in the form, We are victims. They're saying, We're going to get around that some way, but it's not going to be the way you think. We're going to get around it the way most American elites have, by hustling, by stepping outside the law, by shaping the law in our interest, and so forth. And people say, Oh, but that's rather downbeat talk, isn't it? That's not very hopeful. And the young people say, Well, the level of hope is based on the reality.

Now, what do we say back to them? Part of my response has to do with a certain kind of appeal to their moral sense. Part of it has to do with their connection to a tradition, from grandmother to grandfather to father to mother and so forth, that has told them that it is often better to be right and moral as opposed to being simply successful in the cheapest sense. And yet we all know that there must be some victories, some successes, if we're going to keep this tradition alive. If we're to keep alive the King legacy, the grand legacy of yourself, of Paul Robeson, and others, and be able to convince them that what we're talking about is real, what do we say? This is what I struggle with every day.

## Reflecting: Looking into Our Guilt and Shame

Guilt is a very difficult emotion to deal with. Review the definitions earlier in this section that distinguish guilt and shame before starting to think about the following questions. Stay open to your own truth. In itself, guilt is useful only as a motivator to make amends. If irrational, it leads to increased distancing. Each one of us has different ways of dealing with guilt.

Begin looking into guilt and shame by journaling on the following questions in a general way, not specifically addressing whiteness, white privilege, or racism.

1. What does guilt feel like?

_____

_____

_____

_____

_____

_____

_____

2. How do you react to feeling guilty?

_____

_____

_____

_____

_____

_____

_____

3. Have you ever been immobilized by guilt? Describe the situation.

_____

_____

_____

_____

_____

_____

_____

_____

_____

_____

4. Have you ever moved through guilt to positive action? How did you do it?

_____

_____

_____

_____

_____

_____

_____

_____

_____

_____

## Exercises: Clearing the Way

Not everyone carries burdens of guilt or shame, but for those who do, acknowledging and talking about it can be scary. Examining guilt and shame can reactivate the feelings, leaving you feeling uncomfortable and unsafe. During the exercises in this section, remember to be gentle on yourself and recognize the courage it takes to acknowledge any guilt or shame you carry. Also be alert to the anger that shame generates so easily; notice it but don't let it distance you from the process of exploring shame and guilt.

### Stereotypes We Carry

Implementing this group simulation about stereotypes* can help you understand the shame attached to messages you hold from childhood socialization as you experience speaking and hearing stereotypes about various categories of people.

Before you begin, you will prepare small stick-on labels that identify various people from diverse ethnic and racial groups. For example, "African-American male athlete" or "Chinese-American female writer." During the exercise you will form two circles. The inner circle sits in silence, eyes closed, a label on each person's back identifying a racial or ethnic category. Those in the outer circle move from one person in the inner circle to the next, whispering something to the person, based on the label. For example, a label "Asian male college student" might elicit the response, "Are you in computer science?" The purpose of the exercise is to notice what questions and statements come to mind, even if you can see the bias in them. And to experience the feeling of receiving these remarks.

Those who listen will try to guess which category is pinned on their back by analyzing what is said to them. After completing one round, the inner and outer groups will reverse and repeat. After completing both rounds, you will discuss how you felt speaking and how you felt listening.

### Instructions

1.  Prepare enough labels to attach one to each participant. Use categories from the following list to get you started:

| | |
|---|---|
| African-American male lawyer | Native-American male student |
| Chicano female social worker | African-American female housekeeper |
| Chinese-American male salesman | White female production worker |
| White male businessman | Japanese-American female teacher |
| Native-American female writer | Arab-American female artist |
| White female "Valley Girl" student | African-American male student |
| Latino male farm worker | Asian-American female waitress |
| Arab-American male shop keeper | Latino male musician |

2. Divide the group in half and form inner and outer circles, with the inner circle seated.

3. Read these instructions: "The inner group remains seated in silence with eyes closed. Those in the outer circle walk around the perimeter stopping to whisper into the ear of each person, one at a time, saying whatever comes to mind in response to the label on that person's back.

   "When in the outer circle, do not censor, say whatever comes to mind, even if you do not agree with the statement. Do not tell the person what their label is. When in the inner circle, trust the process, focus on what is being said to you."

4. Press labels on those seated.

5. Outer circle walks around once or twice, whispering into the ears of those seated.

6. Read the questions from Step 9 aloud while the inner circle is still seated, but *do not discuss* at this point.

7. Remove labels.

8. Reverse roles and repeat Steps 2-7.

9. Make one big circle and process the activity with the following questions.

   -- How did you feel about this exercise. Was it easy for you to participate? Difficult?

   -- What were some comments made to you? To what comments did you have a strong reaction or response?

   -- Did you figure out your label?

   -- When you were the interviewer, which labels were most difficult to respond to?

   -- What did you learn about the stereotypes of your label? How did it feel? Bring up issues of tokenism, self-fulfilling prophecy, competition between groups, representing your people.

   -- What did you learn from this exercise?

   -- How does this relate to your own real-life label?

-- How does stereotyping affect how you treat others or how others treat you?

-- What do you do when you see stereotypes happen? How might you support other groups?

*Thanks to Carla Trujillo for this exercise.

### The Burden of Guilt

What guilt do you carry from your own interracial interactions? What guilt do you carry from history and your ancestors? For example, a white woman may feel ashamed that she didn't help the young black woman who asked her for directions because she was afraid; she may feel guilty about the genocide of Native Americans in the U.S.

Create a list of examples of the guilt you carry. After creating the list, go back and identify which ones you consider useful guilt and which are irrational guilt. If you have forgotten this distinction, refer to "Rethinking the Role of Guilt and Shame in White Women's Anti-racism Work" earlier in this section.

_____

_____

_____

_____

_____

_____

_____

_____

_____

_____

_____

_____

_____

_____

### Strategies for Reparation

Sitting with a partner, choose a few examples from the list prepared in the previous exercise and begin to brainstorm strategies for reparation or for reducing the burden of irrational guilt. In "Raícism" Morales gives a moving example of how she both reduced the guilt around having slaveholding ancestors and found a way to make reparation for their actions. Take notes on your ideas and be prepared to share them with the group.

*Notes* _____

_____

_____

_____

_____

_____

_____

_____

_____

_____

_____

_____

_____

_____

_____

_____

_____

### Releasing Shame

To conclude the exploration of shame and guilt, you can symbolically release unwanted and burdensome shame. Take a few moments to reflect back on shameful moments in your past—shame from any source, not necessarily related to white privilege or racism. Write down on a separate piece of paper any shame you carry that you want to be rid of. Place the paper in an ashtray or flame proof bowl and burn it. Other alternatives are to tear it up into tiny pieces, or bury the paper in the ground. Do what is significant and meaningful for you. As you symbolically release unwanted and burdensome emotions, tell yourself that you no longer need old shame, that every day you are learning more about how to live up to your own ideals.

# Section VI

# *ACTION*

## Breaking Through into Action

In previous sections of this book your journey has taken you down many different learning paths. You've learned how white people automatically benefit from white privilege at the expense of people of color. You've seen how shielded people are from the information that would help them understand the social systems that keep people divided along race and class lines. Finally, you've examined how fear and guilt help perpetuate racism and white privilege and deny genuine relationships between white people and people of color. The unspoken assumption throughout is that provided with this information, you will be moved to act — moved to begin unraveling racism.

Now you are ready to consider the variety of ways in which we can confront racist systems, joining the struggle for true social equality and justice. A fundamental question for white people is why do it? Why work to end white privilege? Several readings touch on this question. Fundamentally, everyone benefits. Without a commitment to ending white privilege and working to end racism, no one will experience beloved community, first imagined by Martin Luther King, Jr. No one will live in a society where they can be fully who they are.

Ignoring or denying the evidence of racism and white privilege we see around us every day distorts our own lives. It deprives us of a world created by many different people sharing power and working together. We are also lending our tacit approval of the status quo, helping to perpetuate a racist system.

The more you learn about racism and white privilege, the more entrenched and pervasive you can see they are. How can you hope to challenge such a monumental social structure? By making racism seem too big to change, we give ourselves an excuse for doing nothing. As bell hooks writes, "No responsibility need be taken for not changing something if it is perceived as immutable."

The unjust systems of racism are not immutable. You can undertake action in many arenas. Indeed, this journey requires it. The reflective work you do to understand how you unconsciously support oppressive systems begins the personal transformation process. You become aware and accountable in regard to any white privilege you carry. You can then begin to repattern yourself, changing from the inside out. In the community, action can involve patiently and stubbornly working to build meaningful interpersonal relationships across racial boundaries, breaking through the walls that keep us from one another. Action also means confronting, resisting, and dismantling institutionalized racism, whether on the job or in your children's school.

The writings that follow show how ordinary people have taken action, from small daily acts to participating in large, organized movements. Telling the truth, speaking back to power, listening to the oppressed, replacing anger with love, permitting ourselves to be vulnerable—all are ways to engage in unraveling racism. A small group of people can change the world.

## Readings: Many Paths on the Journey

There's no single way to dismantle racism, nor do activists necessarily agree on effective anti-racism strategies. The readings explore a variety of approaches:

- We need to develop sharper critiques of racism and white supremacy that grow from the pain of telling it like it is, says Joy James in "Truth Telling."

- Charlayne Hunter-Gault talks about how journalists and others who report news for the media can take responsibility for confronting racist bias and stereotyping in a conversation in *Restoring Hope* by Cornel West.

- "In a Room with a Bunch of White Guys" by Bill Proudman examines how white men are hurt by oppression and what they need from each other in order to work against racism and sexism.

- For white people, is building personal relationships with people of color sufficient to dismantle racism? Why should white people confront racism? Noel Ignatiev and William "Upski" Wimsatt argue these questions in an excerpt from "I'm Ofay, You're Ofay" by Cornel West.

- In "What I've Learned About Undoing Racism" Andrea Ayvazian outlines her history of anti-racism work and shares insights into what's important.

## *Truth Telling*

*Because women can retreat to a women's community as a safe space, we may hesitate to bring up potentially divisive issues. However, without honesty, community is unrealized. Joy James discusses the necessity of truth telling, especially around the crucial issue of race.* From Joy James, "Truth Telling" from *Skin Deep: Women Writing on Color, Culture, and Identity*, edited by Elena Featherston, 1994, The Crossing Press, p. 70. Copyright (c) 1994 The Crossing Press. Source: The Crossing Press. Joy James teaches womanist theory and courses on African American women and liberation movements at the University of Massachusetts at Amherst.

A certain level of honesty should be the ground on which we stand. That involves the pain of truth telling, even saying things to each other that appear to be divisive. Being honest with each other is very much a matter of revealing our flaws and telling the ways in which we rub each other the wrong way so that we can fit together as a community

Part of the truth telling is, for me, that the crucial issue remains "race." Of course, sexuality, class, gender, and religion are all important components of our present social conditions, but I believe that race will be the crucial issue as we enter the twenty-first century as it continues to shape our sexual, class, and gender experiences.

If we look globally at the destruction of community and the disappearance of cultures, this process very much remains racialized, and that is part of our inheritance. So if we are to function as a community, I would like to see us challenge that inheritance in a very radical fashion. That means not only that we need to develop sharper critiques of racism and white supremacy, and the ways in which they assault every community in every culture and all women, but that we also need to challenge caste systems that exist among ourselves. This requires that we have a loving commitment to radicalism. I am committed to ruthless struggle, but I don't want to become so committed that I forget the humane side. I try to remember that radical change, or the uprooting process, is not about controlling anything.

When I have political fights with other women about racism, it is sometimes very hard to remember that we all belong to one human community. The sheer arrogance and insolence I encounter amazes me sometimes, and the only way I can keep from being overwhelmed by bitterness and from refusing to join in communities with women "as women" is by going back to an idea of struggle where love is the center. But that doesn't mean taking abuse from people. It means that you tell the truth no matter what, and you struggle with such principle that you never allow yourself to disrespect your opponent's humanity. You have to respect your opponent's humanity; you remain linked to her or him.

I have found that, while it is easy to dismiss my opponent's humanity and use that heightened anger and that "moral justification" to push things through, anger is not the best energy to work with if it doesn't have a loving perspective. You can be just as principled by accepting the humanity of people who are destructive, who are arrogant, who act as if they were born to rule, while opposing that kind of behavior by the strength that loving gives you, if you can tap into it.

A very important aspect of the idea of community is that you can't learn this loving in isolation. You really can only learn this kind of loving when it is not easy. It is almost as if through struggle you learn love that is reconciliation without acquiescence. This requires understanding the lay of the land and then doing what is necessary to change the terrain, to change the landscape and make it more habitable for human beings.

A women's community apart from the community at large is a social construction that can become a retreat. Women who feel that they have nowhere else to go may not challenge each other, in order not to lose the only community they have. One cannot form anything truly revolutionary in the communities' outlook and loving in the most uncompromising fashion, out of desperation or retreat. You would compromise to maintain that association or "community."

Our political ideologies as women reflect the span of political ideologies in this society, from Nazi to progressive revolutionary. I am very careful where I walk and with whom I form coalitions or community. The point is not to lose your energy in trying to sustain something that may not have roots, that may be like weeds growing with very shallow roots.

This culture is becoming increasingly violent, and I see our choices narrowing. It is a matter of getting to our feet and acting quickly because there is less leeway and less time to make mistakes. And in this process, women will self-select. Not every woman or every group of women will find that the benefits of a democratic space outweigh the elitist privileges they get from climbing a little higher up in the hierarchies of society.

What is rooted, what grows deep, will transcend women's community. All our different cultures and spiritual practices speak to what that community is. It is a community that transcends gender and all the different ways in which we have been socialized to think in compartments.

### *Charlayne Hunter-Gault and Cornel West on Restoring Hope*

Restoring Hope: Conversations on the Future of Black America *records conversations between Cornel West and various fascinating figures working in politics, religion, and the arts in the U.S. The following excerpt is from the conversation with Charlayne Hunter-Gault, a journalist with extensive experience as an investigative reporter and in TV news. She has worked for the New York Times and The MacNeil/Lehrer Report, among others. In this conversation she talks about how the media perpetuates stereotypes and how a responsible reporter can challenge that tendency.* From Charlayne Hunter-Gault and Cornel West, *Restoring Hope: Conversations on the Future of Black America* by Cornel West and Kevin Shawn Sealey, 1997, pp. 66-67. Copyright © 1997 Beacon Press, Boston. Source: Beacon Press, Boston.

CHG: Well, I think that the mass media emphasize and exacerbate the negative. But what I was about to say is that in spite of the magnification of the negative and the aberrational and the bizarre and the sensational, I think that there's still a critical mass of young people out there who do give us hope. I see them, and I know you do all the time on college campuses. The kids who are being portrayed on television as predators are not the kids who are coming to see Cornel West lecture on a college campus or in a black community. Those are the kids who give us hope, who give me hope. And that is why I don't despair. Now, I do despair sometimes about our inability to reach into the psyche of people who still feel superior to black people, who still feel manipulative toward black people, and also into the psyche of black people who have allowed white people to make them feel as if they are second-class citizens. Those things I despair about. But at the same time I see enough on the positive side, the glass-half-full side, that I do not yet despair.

CW: I tell you, it's good to hear someone like you who does have a certain confidence and faith in much of the younger generation. You hear them trashed all the time.

CHG: I just am out there. You know, these people who are trashing the younger generation are like a lot of editors who sit in newsrooms and dream up things for reporters to do that are not based in reality. There is some sort of intellectual exercise that these editors go through, but they don't live there, ain't been there, don't know them, ain't done that. So they'll tell a reporter, go out and tell us how bad things are in such and such a place. The good reporters either say right there on the spot, You've got the wrong idea about this, or accept the assignment, say nothing, and come back and tell them what they saw. Now, those who are ambitious and have no principles will go out and bring the editor back exactly what he or she asked for because they see that as the way to get ahead. But if you're going to come back with the truth, and the truth is different from what you were sent to pursue, you've got to bring your facts with you and be strong enough to convince that editor that the idea might have got you going but that it was wrong. And here is the truth. And it's tough. That's probably why you don't see more reporting of the positive side. It's because of the gatekeepers in our industry, the media, as well as in corporate America—

CW And in the academy.

CHG: And in the academy and every other institution of this society that is still predominantly white and predominantly male. There's nothing wrong with being white; there's nothing wrong with being male. Some of my best friends are both. But if you are going to transmit images and portray people and have the power of the communications media—especially television, although print does its own share of negative imagery and portrayal—you've got to have some personal experience in order to be fair. And this is where diversity comes in—not as a Christian concept of being fair and all of that, but as a business principle. You have to have people who see things differently so that, in the intellectual mix, you can come out with a better representation of what you're dealing with, if you're honest. Some of these organizations do have black people in them and Hispanic people or gay people or women. But when those people try to present a different perspective, they're not listened to. They're just dismissed. But you can't dismiss somebody who insists on being heard.

CW: I know that's true.

### In a Room with a Bunch of White Guys

*Bill Proudman believes it's necessary for white men to come together to look at how they can eliminate racism and sexism. In this excerpt he answers some of his own questions regarding why do this work and what makes it possible. "In a Room with a Bunch of White Guys" by Bill Proudman was published in* Zip Lines, *Spring 1998.*

Often in workshops I ask white male participants to respond to a series of open-ended questions as a way of bearing witness to each of our ongoing processes.

The statements vary from session to session but sometimes include:

- What I want you to know about me is...

- A next step for me with other white men in the process of building sustainable inclusive organization is...

- A block or barrier that gets in my way of connecting with other white men is...

- Some help and support I need from other white men is...

I decided it might be appropriate in an article about white men and diversity to answer these statements myself as a way of furthering dialogue on these topics.

**What I want you to know about me is...**

- That I am working hard to understand and celebrate my cultural heritage and family roots and that in doing so I can reclaim more of my sense of feeling personally grounded. Often, when I ask white people, and white men in particular, to talk about their ethnicity as best they currently understand it, I am met with blank stares or answers such as, "I'm an American," "Southerner," "Texan" or, even worse, "Heinz 57," "a mutt," etc. For many white Americans, the notion of ethnicity is something that is largely the domain of folks of color. I have grown increasingly intrigued as to why we either are unable to answer or do so in terms that are less than celebratory. One of the reasons that we as white people haven't had to think much about our heritage is because of the vestiges we receive from white privilege. Comments from white people like "I don't see people as black and white, I treat everyone the same" further reinforce the effect of white privilege to make difference invisible, when racial difference has been and continues to be a very significant factor in discrimination.

I believe one of the ways I can assist in dismantling racism is to take full ownership and pride in my ethnic background. While I struggle with many family secrets that hide the truth on this question, my search has revealed more personal understanding about me and my ancestors and our own travels to this continent. My mother is adopted, and at present we are in search of her blood lines. My father's ancestors came over to this country in the bowels of a boat as stowaways and apparently changed the family name to Proud man from Broudman (descendants of the British Isles). I find in my own search that the lines are hazy and many of my relatives have dismissed such searching and instead view themselves as Americans. The search continues and with it the undoing of new layers of both family pride and pain. It is an unfolding process.

- That I am committed to not giving up on anyone, starting with myself and other white men. I am particularly focused on engaging other white men to do the necessary work around our conditioned disconnect from ourselves and each other, which at times (for me) is disguised as self-competence and self-confidence.

- That I view this work as both vital and fun and that I have learned to expand my previous definition of fun.

- That I am also in process and in this learning for the long haul. There are no quick fixes here or simple answers to vexing questions. I have found that in asking questions I have usually ended up with ever more questions rather than definitive answers. Just because I facilitate on issues of difference and inclusion does not mean I have worked through all my conditioning as a white man.

- That when I facilitate a group of white men, I cannot hide behind the mask of facilitator. That if I do hide and not allow my stuff to come out, this very action gives the other men present the opportunity to disconnect their heads from their hearts. I continue to see the strengthening of my relationship with other white men as an integral part of the larger process of interrupting and eliminating all forms of oppression in our society. I have found that my journey as a facilitator is one of constant growth and change.

One pivotal point came last year when I was planning the first three-day workshop designed exclusively for white men focusing on racism, sexism and homophobia. I realized that if I facilitated that gathering the way I had always thought of facilitation it just would not work for participants. So I decided to invite my father to participate in the workshop as a way to keep myself engaged and immersed in my stuff as a white man. His presence provided me with the recurring impetus to keep my head fully connected to my heart and soul and not detach. That decision caused a major breakthrough for me both as a facilitator and as a white man continuing to do my own work. This powerful and wonderful experience forever changed how I viewed my role as facilitator. Tops on my list is the letting go of a set of absolute facilitator dos and don'ts. Being present and real with people I was facilitating has taken on a whole new meaning. This moment has acted to unleash a continuing wave of new "ahas" about how I can be present, facilitate thoughtfully and serve my clients.

- My full liberation as a person is not complete while there exists any form of racism, sexism, heterosexism, ableism and any other form of systemic oppression. My liberation is an unfolding and continuing process, not a one-stop destination.

- That while these topics are large and often overwhelming, the sheer magnitude of the undertaking does not change my ability to choose on a case-by-case basis how I wish to interact with people at any given time.

- That my learning is endless. That when I think there is a plateau to my learning and understanding about race, gender and difference, I become my own worst barrier to expanding my learning and understanding.

**A next step for me with other white men in the process of building sustainable inclusive organization is...**

- To consciously work with other white men to interrupt the lies and misinformation we have learned about ourselves, other white men, women and folks of color.

- To go after all white men from a place of compassion and heart in the deep belief that we have important work to do together just as we have equally important work to do with the female and of color colleagues we work and live with.

- To continue to be open and aware of how I continue to grow and change.

**A block or barrier that gets in my way of connecting with other white men is...**

- My fear of white men (or maybe myself) in appearing less than, not competent or not capable (sort of like being afraid to ask for directions) so that this fear acts to paralyze me into silent inaction.

- My assumed need to maintain control of my emotions, actions, outcomes or my vulnerability.

**Some help and support I need from other white men is...**

- To recognize that I can't do this by myself even though my white male conditioning has taught me to think that I can.

- To be present and aware of their actions and behaviors.

- To not give up on any of us. That together, we can undo much of what we have learned and be active allies with other white men and women and folks of color to create new organizational cultures that bring out the very best in all of us.

- To be willing to do the work, each at our own speed and in our own way. There are multiple paths towards moving in a desired direction.

- To not target others, including white men, as the enemy in order to establish some form of "us versus them" solidarity.

### I'm Ofay, You're Ofay (excerpt)

*"What's a white person to do?" In the following excerpts, Cornel West, professor of philosophy of religion and Afro-American studies at Harvard University, white hip-hopper William "Upski" Wimsatt, and Noel Ignatiev, who pioneered whiteness studies and wants to abolish whiteness, talk and argue over what is to be done about the white race.* From Cornel West "I'm Ofay, You're Ofay" in *Transition: An International Review*, Vol. 73, "The White Issue," pp. 176-178 and 182-187. Copyright (c) University Press. Source: Duke University Press.

What's a white person to do? That is, as the white girl once asked of Malcolm X, what can a sincere white person do to help? Although the answer seemed obscure to Malcolm at the time, his ultimate response, as told to Alex Haley—go and fight racism among your own—was to the point. While Malcolm had his misgivings about whites and blacks working together, there have been, of course, numerous white fighters in the black freedom struggle.

The list of whites who participated in the fight to overcome black misery is longer than most of us suspect, and it spans the centuries: George Keith, whose letter to his fellow Quakers is the earliest surviving written protest against black slavery in the US.; the inimitable John Brown; William Lloyd Garrison, editor of the *Liberator*; abolitionist writers and orators including Lydia Maria Child, Wendell Phillips, and Elijah Lovejoy; civil rights activists like John Jay Chapman, Anne Braden, Myles Horton, Palmer Weber, and Virginia Durr; radical historians including Herbert Aptheker and Eric Foner; radical journalists and editors like Paul Sweezy, Carey McWilliams, and Harry Magdoff. Still, this grand caravan of courageous white Americans is a marginal tradition. The fight against white supremacy has never been a priority for the vast majority of white people in this country.

At issue, I would argue, is the enduring power and pervasiveness of white racism. Most whites fail to see its aesthetic, social, psychological, and economic ramifications. Even those whites struggling to end racism tend to think narrowly, making individualistic moral appeals. The tenacity of white racism can inspire a powerful fear, a fear that can only be overcome by a fundamental transformation in one's view of oneself. Full-fledged affirmation of the humanity of black, red, yellow, and brown people requires a conversion that turns the world upside down, forcing one to confront just how deep white supremacy still lurks in the inner recesses of one's own soul.

This is a lonely and difficult road, especially in the absence of the kinds of powerful multiracial organizations of yesteryear—trade unions, ecumenical religious groups, and civil rights groups. Most white citizens find it difficult to believe that a substantive and serious struggle against white racism is possible.

The major problem confronting our courageous white contemporaries in the struggle—antiracists such as David Montgomery and Letty Cottin Pogrebin, as well as "abolitionists" like Noel Ignatiev, John Garvey, and David Roediger—is how to create circumstances that can reveal the depths of white supremacy to people in such a way as to enable them to fight this evil, in their society and in their souls. This life-transforming process requires moral vision, resoluteness, and communal support, but also a social and political movement led by those willing to die to overcome the suffering of people of color—and thereby secure the freedom of us all.

I recently met with representatives of two very different generations of white radical activists, men with very different relationships to theory, practice, and black culture. Both of them have put themselves—or their white skin, as they might say—on the line for their beliefs.

William " Upski" Wimsatt is a young Chicago-based writer and former graffiti artist—a white boy from the South Side of Chicago, and a self-professed (and self-critical) "wigger," to boot. He is the author of one of the most controversial pieces in hip-hop journalism history—an essay for the *Source* entitled "We Use Words Like Mack-adocious," an attack on white hip-hop fans who don't know any black people. He is also the author of "In Defense of Wiggers" [In *Transition* #73] and *Bomb the Suburbs*, a self-published anthology of writings on rap, race, and activism. His charisma stems from his courage: the "book tour" for *Bomb the Suburbs* took the form of a "bet with America." Upski surveyed whites about the "worst parts" of inner-city areas across urban America—and went to them. If he lived, he said, whites should think twice about their studied avoidance of urban areas, and maybe even think about moving to them.

Noel Ignatiev worked in the labor movement in Chicago for decades until coming to Harvard University in 1986 to pursue a degree in American civilization. His Ph.D. dissertation was published by Routledge in 1994 as *How the Irish Became White*, an attempt to describe the process of Americanization as an accommodation to "whiteness"—how immigrants become American by distancing themselves from blacks, thereby achieving the privileges that accrue to white skin. Ignatiev helped pioneer the scholarly study of whiteness, but his primary interest is not to study whiteness but to "abolish" it. He is coeditor (with John Garvey) of the hard-to-find magazine *Race Traitor* and the book *Race Traitor Anthology*. His *Race Traitor Manifesto* will appear later this year.

In a sprawling, combative, sometimes vituperative conversation earlier this year, the three of us wrangled over how best to involve white people in the fight against racism and inequality.

*[After some discussion about various approaches to ending racism, all agree any approach needs to have some "teeth" behind it.]*

WW: That's what I want to get into, what some of those teeth might be. First of all, white people need to admit, straight up, our racism. It's not enough to just say, "Yeah, we have some racism deep within us." Then there are the basic personal choices one makes in life. Who's in your family? Who's in your extended family? Who are your friends? Who are your closest friends? Do they reflect the whole range of people in America? Do they reflect the whole spectrum of people within each of those races? If you have black friends, does that include rich and poor, male and female? Does it include the whole mix of black people, or can you only deal with a certain kind of black person? What are the power relationships within those friendships? What do you tell each other and what don't you tell each other? This is just the beginning. And then that moves into, Where do you live? How do you make your money? Who do you make your money off of? Because a lot of the cool white people are making their money off of black folks. And how do you spend your money? If you make $80,000 a year and the average annual income is $30,000, what's stopping you from living on $30,000, and putting the rest of the money into community based organizations . . . into *Race Traitor*, into efforts that are underfunded as hell, that need that money. This is not—

NI: Let's talk about something else.

WW. OK.

NI: See, I appreciate the compliments you paid me [earlier in the conversation] on my genuineness and so on, but I don't think I deserve any particular credit for working in the steel mills for twenty years or for living on the West Side of Chicago. Millions of people work in steel mills and live on the West Side of Chicago. They don't get any particular credit for it, and I don't claim any either. I understand that you want to judge people by what they do rather than merely by what they say, but you also need to ask whether they are willing to challenge and to come into conflict with white people, other white people. I do not frankly believe that choosing, as a white individual, to live in a black neighborhood or to have black friends is particularly dangerous to anyone.

WW: Then why do few white people do it?

NI: Because it's not comfortable. Many do it as a form of flight. There was a whole movement in the '60s of people who pulled themselves out, withdrew from the official institutions of society, and went off and built their own societies. They represented no alternative and no challenge.

CW: Communes.

NI: Yeah. You're not going to build an island of the future society within this hell of the reality.

WW: You think I'm saying that?

NI: Yes. Or at least you're not saying anything beyond that. The test is the willingness to confront, challenge, and provoke opposition, to oppose the institutions that are reproducing race as a social category. And one can do that from wherever one lives. One can do that from North Dakota and Montana, where there's not a black person within five hundred miles. You don't need to be friends with black folks to hate white supremacy and oppose it. Certainly, if you have black friends, you learn things, you gain strength, it makes your life richer, and so forth and so on. All that is true. But that's not the test. The test is a willingness to confront the institutions that exist in society. I mean, *Race Traitor* doesn't need the money. We sell enough copies to publish. This, to me, is the test, wherever you are: do you fight so hard against the barriers that exclude black people, against the barriers of white supremacy, that either you win and those barriers come down, or you are such a nuisance to the white people that they kick you out of those suburbs? That, to me, is the test. Not, "Do you choose to live in the inner city?" but "Do you fight so hard to bust open that white suburb that they won't let you live there anymore?"

WW: Is that a prescription for me?

NI: For everyone, in general. I can't speak to you specifically, but it's for everyone. I mean, yes, white folks need black friends, because they learn from them, but that, by itself, is only like admiring hip-hop music.

WW: What!

NI: It's on the level of admiring and appreciating hip-hop music. It's a potential for something, but by itself, it isn't that thing, because it does not, by itself, represent a challenge to the institutions of white supremacy. When I worked in the factories, the guys, black and white, hung around together on the job and they were friendly, but I remember saying to one of the guys, "Next week, we're going to get together over at Munroe's house for a picnic, and the week after that, we're going to get together over at your house in the suburbs." And he says, "Well, hold on." He had black friends and he appreciated soul and all that, but he was not willing to challenge his neighbors and jeopardize his position, so it didn't mean anything.

WW: How many white people do you know who you've seen do this, who you've seen challenge or—

NI: I've known many who have done it in little ways, in small episodic—

WW: How many of them did not have deep relationships with black people?

NI: Upski! I'm not arguing against deep relationships with black people! I sat here while you listed three or four things, including deep relationships with black people—which I cherish and do my best to maintain—but you never got around to talking about challenging the institutions of white supremacy. For you, friendships, who your friends are and so forth, became the test. For me, it's not the test, it's just a step on the path to getting ready for the test.

CW: I think one way of talking about it is that there is a long tradition in the United States of perceiving the vicious legacy of white supremacy through individualistic and moralistic lenses. You know you hate it, and you're going to reach out. You know you hate it, but you want some kind of relation with the folk catching hell. You know you hate it, but you want to clean and clear your own conscience. You know you hate it, so you want to make sure that somehow you're not tainted with its ugliness, and therefore you can just dip in blackness. But that's not a political commitment, that's a moralistic move. It's not evil; it's just that it doesn't go far enough.

NI: I would even go a little further than that, because I'm not going to let Upski off the hook so easily. See, when I talk to these white folks, I want to talk to them not about blackness—they don't know anything about blackness and I only know a little bit. I want to talk to them about whiteness, which is a subject I am an expert on, having spent all my conscious life doing battle against it. I want to talk to them about what it means to be white, what they gain from it and what it costs them, what they think they are, and what they might be as an alternative. Then, once that is stirred up, once they start to think, "Wait a minute. This ain't such a great deal after all. There are costs I never thought about," then they'll find ways of doing battle against whiteness. My observation has always been, in my years in the factories and so forth, that any time a white person challenged white supremacy, challenged the supremacist job classifications and all the rest of the stuff, with or without any advance discussion with black people, the black folks would always find a way of expressing their gratitude, their solidarity, their friendship, and their support. They would go out of their way to do that kind of thing. Certainly you can learn a tremendous amount from black folk, but the point I keep making is that fighting whiteness is not something that we do as a favor to black people.

WW: Am I saying that?

NI: No, but some people are. This is not something that we do as a favor to black people. Everybody in this country who wants to be free has as much reason as anybody else to destroy white supremacy. It's the enemy of all of us.

WW: That's bullshit. A lot of people benefit from it.

NI: I'm talking about people who want to be free. Those who gain the privileges of whiteness renounce their humanity and their universality. Of course we can learn a tremendous amount from the people who have been fighting white supremacy for centuries, even though we just got into it, relatively speaking, last week. But that's not done as a favor to them.

CW: That's true. That's very, very true.

WW: Amen.

NI: If that's all the argument is, then there's no argument.

. . .

### What I've Learned About Undoing Racism

*As an anti-racism trainer, Andrea Ayvazian, has spent years working to disman-*
*tle racism. In this article she shares stories from her own journey, discusses com-*
*mon obstacles for white people who want to work against racism, and offers some*
*suggestions from her own experience for unlearning racism personally and work-*
*ing to transform racist institutions.* From Andrea Ayvazian, "What I've
Learned About Undoing Racism," in Peacework, November 1990. Copyright (c) 1990 American Friends Service Committee. Reprinted by permis-
sions of Peacework magazine, a publication of The American Friends
Service Committee.

I remember the first Unlearning Racism Workshop I attended, over
a decade ago. I can picture myself in the predominately white
group, everyone gathered in a circle. I remember feeling self-con-
scious, guilty, fearful, and cautious lest I say the wrong thing and
thus appear racist. The mental image I retain of my presence that
day is of me sitting with my arms and legs crossed, my brow knitted
together in a tight and pensive look—my whole body fortressed, my
mind sharp and ready to monitor my speech and defend my
actions.

It was a difficult day for me: I resisted and rebelled. The armor I
used to keep the issues at arm's length was my hypercritical self. I
managed to find fault with almost everything the trainers presented, thereby making myself somewhat superior and impervious
to their points. I struggled with them. But more sunk in and took
hold than I realized. Bits of their presentation would rattle around
inside for me some time to come.

I did not realize then how much that day was a beginning for me, a
baptism of sorts. I was starting on a a journey. Since then, events and
decisions have propelled me forward—quietly and nervously at
first, but forward nonetheless—to work on issue of oppression, and
especially on racism.

Sometimes we have a sensation that we have been called to do
something—not with thunder and lightning, but with a whisper
from within. For me, the whisper was barely audible ten years
ago—but it grew in volume and clarity, and I have been able to "follow a leading," as Quakers say, to speak, teach, and wrestle with
others on issues of racism and white privilege.

For the past five years, I have been leading workshops on Unlearning Racism. I have been the trainer perched in front of the group coaxing other white people to confront the issue of racism. I have had to deal with participants' resistance. I have been the target of their rebellion, and I have had to look at crossed arms and knitted brows. Some days I have ended a workshop feeling hopeless and thinking to myself that I alienated more people than I touched—that folks *say* they want to work on these issues but they don't—and that I hate this work anyway. But some days I have packed up my materials and headed home feeling renewed hope—that we did get somewhere, and that folks like us can and will change the world.

Over the years of attending and leading Unlearning Racism workshops, I have observed certain patterns emerging among white participants and with predominately white groups.

- I have noticed in numerous settings that white people often spend considerable time and energy doing battle with the basic definition of racism now used in most anti-racism workshops, that is "racism equals Social Power plus Prejudice." This concept serves as a cornerstone for the work that follows. It is interesting to discover how much argument this simple definition often causes in groups. White people work hard explaining how little social power they have, defending their status as ordinary individuals with no special advantages or benefits in society. These discussions can become quite passionate. However, it ignores Institutional racism and white privilege. These two concepts are tough ones for some whites to hear and accept.

- Another issue arises around the "Power plus Prejudice" definition, which causes considerable distress, in that it precludes people of color from being racist because they have limited social power in a white-dominated society. (People of color may be prejudiced, some may have ugly feelings about folks in other ethnic groups, but they are not racist.) White people can spend the entire first hour of a workshop explaining why people of color can be and are racist. This argument must bring some relief to the guilt that surfaces when white people look directly at racism, confront it as a *white* problem, and start to wrestle with it.

- Beneath the struggle that erupts over the definition of racism is the difficulty many whites seem to have in accepting the degree of privilege that white skin brings. Asking white people to become aware of their privilege as whites seems to be like asking fish to become aware of water: it is all around us and yet very difficult to see. Racism, a system of advantage based on race, bestows advantages on white people *daily*—privileges and advantages given without our asking and often received without our being aware of it. We live in a very racist society—most whites agree with that point. But grasping the subtle yet profound level of privilege that each white individual has received throughout her/his life is difficult for many folks to absorb.

- Another pattern I have seen emerge is the number of well intentioned groups, deeply committed to working on issues of racism that deal with the topic by designing programs focused on the targeted group—people of color—rather than on the dominant group—white people—as the source of the problem. Striving to be inclusive and overvaluing "dialogue," whites attempt to put people of color under the microscope as a way of solving their own white racism. White people need to work with other white people an our racism. People of color have a role to play in dismantling racism, but it is not in showing us white people the way, forever being our teachers on this issue.

Racism is a white issue and white people need to work together to confront it directly and move to a place where we can be active agents of change. A parallel can be made to sexism. Sexism is an issue that men must address—women are the victims of sexism, not the cause. Women cannot serve as teachers and experts on sexism for men to work out their issues. Women's work is our own liberation and empowerment—and the same is true of people of color. (In fact, people of color often do gather together to work on issues of internalized oppression.)

- Another issue that hampers our forward movement toward dismantling racism is the belief that one-time experiences—even when they are emotionally powerful and full of insights—can transform individuals or organizations. Unlearning personal racism and working towards the dismantling of institutional racism require long-term plans, sustained vigilance, and "daily practice" (as one participant explained it). Too often, groups look for or hope for a quick fix—a single workshop or a dramatic event that will solve the problem in one fell swoop.

Racism is learned and it can be unlearned, but it takes a commitment to stay aware, to keep working, and to accept the unlearning as a life-long journey. White people absorbed racist images and messages early on in life—in schools, houses of worship, children's books, through television, and through our cities and neighborhoods. Clearing out the distorted images and stereotypes we absorbed as children and replacing the misinformation with accurate information requires time and attention— it does not just happen, and it does not happen quickly. Examining the racism inherent in the institutions we are a part of and analyzing how those institutions maintain their whiteness also takes time and focused attention. There am no quick fixes.

Once on the road to liberation. we see that the journey stretches out far ahead. Because we live in a racist society, we are seduced into looking the other way, losing our attention and slipping back into business as usual. But there is no such thing as a passive anti-racist. Business as usual, or quietly complying with the status quo, means colluding with a racist society.

A trainer of color, with whom I worked to prepare myself to lead these workshops, once told me that of all the things that I could teach white people, the single most important concept to convey in my work was to help whites understand that the key to dismantling racism is to "keep paying attention." Keep paying attention to the racism that pervades our society. It is so tempting for white people to pay attention for a while, to attend a workshop, and to think "Work on dismantling racism? I *did* that." We must remember our charge: to keep paying attention, and then say instead: "Work on dismantling racism? I *do* that."

## Reflecting: Thinking Back and Looking Forward

Having nearly completed this workbook, think about the following questions and make some notes.

1. What did this journey stir up in you?

_____

_____

_____

_____

_____

2. Which of the issues that you read about and reflected on do you need to explore more deeply?

_____

_____

_____

_____

3. What are some ways you can work to dismantle racism in your personal relationships and as a social activist?

_____

_____

_____

_____

_____

_____

## Exercises: Finding Our Own Path

It's time for you to take stock of where you've been and look ahead to how you can continue the journey. What are the barriers to continuing this journey? How can you move through them? Are you ready to make a commitment to exposing white privilege and working to dismantle racist systems as you move through your daily life?

## *Barriers to Action*

In learning about white privilege, fear, and guilt you touched on some of the many ways in which you can be held back from right action. Now take some time to try to list all the barriers—external and internal—that can get in the way of anti-racist struggle. For example "I'm overcome by inertia," "I don't know what to do," or "I'm afraid I'll lose my job."

*Notes* _____

_____

_____

_____

_____

_____

_____

_____

_____

_____

_____

_____

_____

_____

_____

_____

_____

_____

_____

### Preparing to Act

Thinking back to the readings, discuss with a partner the questions below.

1. Do you feel capable of the commitment to honesty that several writers believe anti-racist struggle requires? What are some examples of honesty (verbal honesty may not be the only kind of honesty).

_____

_____

_____

_____

_____

_____

_____

2. What is your reaction to being urged to celebrate and welcome difference instead of looking for commonalities?

_____

_____

_____

_____

_____

_____

_____

_____

3. Do you see a difference between personal and political action? Describe both political and personal action.

_____

_____

_____

_____

_____

_____

_____

_____

_____

4. Do white people have to come into conflict with other white people in order to dismantle racism?

_____

_____

_____

_____

_____

_____

_____

_____

_____

_____

### *Moving Through Barriers*

Looking back at the list of barriers, strategize ways to move through them. For every barrier listed, identify at least one strategy for taking action. For example, "be willing to make mistakes" may be a strategy for taking action in spite of "not knowing what to do."

*Notes* _____

_____

_____

_____

_____

_____

_____

_____

_____

_____

_____

_____

_____

_____

_____

_____

_____

_____

### Commitment to Action

What changes could you make in your life over the next few months to continue the journey into understanding whiteness and unraveling racism? For example, read critically, noticing how white people are characterized in comparison to people of color. What are some larger actions you could take? For example, if you are white, hold a series of in-home meetings with some white friends to discuss how to use white privilege to be better allies to people of color in your community.

Make a list of the next possible steps in your journey. After completing your list, choose two actions—one small, daily action and one larger action— to commit to. State your commitments aloud to a friend to affirm your intention. Write the two actions down on a separate piece of paper and post them where they are visible to you every day. Revisit your list regularly and continue to incorporate other actions into your daily life.

*Notes* _____

_____

_____

_____

_____

_____

_____

_____

_____

_____

_____

_____

## Congratulations

Again, welcome to the work, and to one of the most important journeys you will ever undertake. You join an ever-increasing number of people who are concerned about continued dominance of a white culture-oriented society that doesn't provide for equal access to people of color. Not only do people of color not have access to the same privileges of life in the U.S. as those of white European descent, but our country fails to benefit sufficiently from the contributions of its diverse population. Throughout this course, your individual and group explorations of whiteness, white privileges, and racism gave you tools to better understand the world we live in. Even if you do not take on consistent, specific actions (but we hope you do), you have the seeds for a new consciousness.

Perhaps you will have a keener awareness of media reporting or portrayal around people of color. Perhaps you will break silence when you no longer want to go along with the racial stereotypes and humor that are casually accepted around you. Perhaps when you notice the lack of representation of people in groups you participate in, you will be moved to act. The new consciousness you are developing and any supporting actions, no matter how small, do make a difference.

You may choose to continue the work in an affiliation group. White people can work together to understand white privilege, educate themselves around racism, and face their own guilt, shame, and fear. People of color may want to continue healing the deep wounds of racism amongst themselves. We can support these sanctuaries, while remaining available for any opportunities of coming together. In any situation where trust has been broken, we must be patient. White people in particular must continue to prove their willingness to change the status quo, learn how to be good allies, and work with other whites to expand the circle of safety for coming together. Nearly impossible to do alone, diversity work flourishes in a collaborative, cooperative, intentional culture.

Urge any group you are a part of to address inclusivity as an organization. You have a key role in accomplishing any organizational change. Individuals collectively make an organization change. Change is fraught with danger, with resistance, with fears, as well as excitement. Remember, we are all learners together. It's OK to make mistakes, and to be honest and humble about the struggle to get it right. But we must continue educating ourselves, exposing ourselves to new and often uncomfortable opportunities, speaking our truths, and listening to others. The change has already begun.

Again, welcome to the work.

*ACTION*

# REFERENCES

## Bibliography

This eclectic bibliography offers some of our favorite books that deal, in one way or another, with whiteness, white privilege, and the effects of racism. It is by no means an exhaustive listing of current publications on those topics, and we are noticing that the offerings on whiteness are expanding every day. The titles given range from serious academic works to journalistic essays and from easy-reading novels to soul-searching autobiography.

### *Essays, Analysis, and Anthologies*

*Becoming and Unbecoming White: Owning and Disowning a Racial Identity*, Christine Clark and James O'Donnell, eds. (Bergin & Garvey, 1999). From a variety of viewpoints the contributors address white racialization and what is required to make whites realize that the benefits of being antiracist outweigh the benefits of being racist.

*Black on White: Black Writers on What It Means to Be White*, David R. Roediger, editor (Schocken, 1998). Brings together the work of more than fifty black writers to take a close look at the meaning of whiteness in America.

*Beyond the Whiteness of Whiteness: Memoir of a White Mother of Black Sons*, Jane Lazarre (Duke University Press, 1996). Through maternal reflection, Lazarre confronts the white racism that has shaped American society and challenges white people to move beyond whiteness.

*By the Color of Our Skin: The Illusion of Integration and the Reality of Race*, Leonard Steinhorn and Barbara Diggs-Brown (Dutton, 1999). The authors—one white and the other black—tell us why they believe integration is a myth and how the myth has become so deeply intrenched.

*Colonize This! Young Women of Color on Today's Feminism*, Daisy Hernandez and Bushra Rehman, editors (Seal Press, 2002). Writings that testify to the movement—political and physical—of a new generation of citizens, activists, and artists.

*The Coming Race War? And Other Apocalyptic Tales of America after Affirmative Action and Welfare*, Richard Delgado (New York University Press, 1996). Explores merit and affirmative action; the nature of empathy and false empathy; and the limitations of legal change.

*Half and Half [Writers on Growing Up Biracial + Bicultural]*, Claudine Chiawei O'Hearn, editor (Pantheon, 1998). Eighteen essays address the difficulties of not fitting into and the benefits of being part of two worlds, mapping a new ethnic terrain that transcends racial and cultural division.

*Invisibility Blues: From Pop to Theory*, Michelle Wallace (Verso, 1990). Wonderful essays on wide range of topics related to race and racism.

*Killing Rage*, bell hooks (Henry Holt, 1995). A black, feminist perspective on racism and visions of a world without it.

*The Last Plantation: Color, Conflict, and Identity*, Itabari Njeri (Houghton Mifflin, 1997). Mixed-race identity and color-based identity examined.

*Learning to Be White: Money, Race, and God in America*, Thandeka (Continuum, 2000). Thandeka asks how does a child, unaware of race, come to identify as white and what are the costs and benefits of that identification, both to the core sense of self and in economic and social terms. Offers an excellent study of white shame.

*Medicine Stories: History, Culture, and the Politics of Integrity*, Aurora Levins Morales (South End Press, 1998). Draws connections between the colonization of whole nations, the health of mountainsides, and the abuse of individual women, children, and men, offering the paradigm of integrity as a political model for those who struggle for justice, health, and love.

*Miscegenation Blues: Voices of Mixed Race Women*, Carol Camper, editor (Sister Vision, 1994). Explores mixed race identity, belonging and not belonging—of grappling in two or more worlds and the journey home.

*Names We Call Home: Autobiography on Racial Identity*, Becky Thompson and Sangeeta Tyagi, eds. (Routledge, 1996). Excellent narratives and analysis by white people and people of color on social construction of racial identities and transforming those identities.

*The Possessive Investment in Whiteness: How White People Profit from Identity Politics*, George Lipsitz (Temple University Press, 1998). A valuable historical and logical explanation of how the value of whiteness was put in place and maintains privilege today.

*Promise and a Way of Life [White Antiracist Activism]*, Becky Thompson (University of Minnesota Press, 2001). Interviews with numerous anitracist activists who tell their motivations, experiences, and histories.

*Racism in the Lives of Women: Testimony, Theory, and Guides to Antiracist Practice*, Jeanne Adleman and Gloria Enguîdanos, editors (Harrington Park Press, 1995). Psychological look at racism; excellent insights.

*Restoring Hope: Conversations on the Future of Black America*, Cornel West (Beacon, 1997). Interviews with several fascinating public figures working in politics, the arts, and religion.

*The Rooster's Egg: On the Persistence of Prejudice*, Patricia Williams (Harvard University, 1995). Thought-provoking essays with unexpected insights into prejudice.

*Skin Deep: Women Writing on Color, Culture and Identity*, Elena Featherston, editor (Crossing Press, 1994). Examines colorism, the deep wound at the heart of racism.

*The Social Construction of Whiteness: White Women, Race Matters*, Ruth Frankenberg (University of Minnesota Press, 1993). What does it means to be white, what is white culture?

*Uprooting Racism: How White People Can Work for Justice*, Paul Kivel (New Society Publishers, 1996).

*Warrior Lessons: An Asian American Woman's Journey Into Power*, Phoebe Eng (Pocket Books, 1999). Addresses many issues, including the "good little minority girl" stereotype. A manual of today's woman warrior as she channels her rage and cultivates her power.

*Where the Body Meets Memory: An Odyssey of Race, Sexuality, and Identity*, David Mura (Anchor, 1996). Memoir focusing on how being a "model minority" results in loss of heritage and wholeness for Japanese Americans.

*Where Is Your Body: Race, Class, Gender and the Law*, Mari Matsuda (Beacon, 1996). How the law treats race; legal strategies for dismantling racism.

*White Lies: Race and the Myths of Whiteness*, Maurice Berger (Farrar, Strauss, and Giroux, 1999). Memoir that is also social history and cultural criticism.

*Whiteness of a Different Color: European Immigrants and the Alchemy of Race*, Matthew Frye Jacobson (Harvard University Press, 1998). Argues that race resides not in nature but in the contingencies of politics and culture. In this nation of immigrants "race" has been at the core of civic assimilation.

*Yellow Woman and a Beauty of Spirit*, Leslie Marmon Silko (Touchstone, 1996). Essays on Native American life today.

*Yours in Struggle*, Elly Bulkin, Minnie Bruce Pratt, Barbara Smith (Long Haul Press, 1984). Perspectives on anti-semitism and racism.

*Yurugu: An African-Centered Critique of European Cultural Thought and Behavior*, Marimba Ani (African World Press, 1994. Uses examples from history, European literature, and European critical and philosophical writing to explore the relationship between European culture and white identity.

### Fiction

*The Changlings*, Jo Sinclair (out of print; check the library). Two young girls, Jewish and black, become friends; takes place in the early 1900s in NY.

*Dessa Rose*, Sherley Anne Williams (Berkeley, 1986). The relationship between a slave and a plantation owner.

*The Gettin Place*, Susan Straight (Anchor Books, 1996). A portrait of a family struggling to defend its turf in a changing world.

*Ghost Singer*, Anna Lee Walter (University of New Mexico, 1996). Traditional and contemporary life intersect in this intriguing story revolving around a Native American collection at the Library of Congress.

*Heart Mountain*, Gretel Ehrlich (Penguin, 1988). Historical novel based on the Japanese relocation camp at Heart mountain in Montana.

*House Made of Dawn*, Scott Momaday (Harper and Row, 1966). Home from the Korean war, a young Native American man struggles to live both in the world of his fathers and the modern world of the mid 20th century.

*Mean Spirit*, Linda Hogan (Autheneum, 1991). Oil is discovered on Indian land in Oklahoma in the 1920s, setting off succeeding rounds of crime and suffering. Based on history, this novel ultimately is about survival.

*Obasan*, Joy Kogawa (Godine, 1984). The story of one Japanese-Canadian family during WWII.

*Push*, Sapphire (Knopf, 1996). A young black woman struggles to heal from the past.

*A Short Walk*, Alice Childress (Avon, 1979). Story of a black woman's life from cradle to grave—1900 to 1950.

*Six Out Seven*, Jess Mowry (Doubleday, 1993). Fleeing the oppression of rural Mississippi, thirteen-year old Corbitt lands on the streets of Oakland, where he faces the harsh realities of ghetto life and learns to trust his own strength.

*Tropic of Orange*, Karen Tei Yamashita (Coffee House Press, 1997). A magical realist slices into the L.A. scene with a multicultural perspective. This is what LA looks like today—if we only notice.

*Typical American*, Gish Jen (Plume, 1991). Lai Fu comes to America to study, expecting to return to China, but soon his name is Ralph and he's setting out to make the American dream come true.

*White Girls*, Lynn Lauber (Vintage, 1990) An interracial love affair.

### Autobiography

*Always Running: Gang Days in LA*, Luis Rodriguez (Touchstone, 1994). An account of life in a gang and getting out.

*Bloodlines: Odyssey of a Native Daughter*, Janet Campbell Hale (Harper Perennial, 1993). Finding strength in her Coeur d'Alene heritage, Hale brings her own and her family's history to life through history, storytelling, and remembrance.

*The Color of Water: A Black Man's Tribute to His White Mother*, James McBride (Riverhead Books, 1996). Memoir of a black man raised by a white mother.

*Invisible Privilege: A Memoir About Race, Class, and Gender,* Paula Rothenberg (University of Kansas, 2000). A candid look at the realities of social and academic privilege.

*Ohitika Woman,* Mary Brave Bird (Harper, 1993). Returning to the reservation after Wounded Knee in 1973, Brave Bird struggles to find a place for her feminist beliefs in her Sioux heritage and her Sioux religion in a Christian culture.

*The Hunger of Memory: the Education of Richard Rodriguez,* Richard Rodriguez (Bantam Books, 1983). Explores the costs of assimilation.

*On Gold Mountain: the 100-Year Odyssey of a Chinese-American Family,* Lisa See (St. Martin's Press, 1995). Fascinating family anecdotes and historical details of Chinese immigrant life.

*Pushed Back to Strength: A Black Woman's Journey Home,* Gloria Wade-Gayles (Avon, 1993). Inspiring chronicle of one woman's travels through intolerance, activism, pain, self-realization, and love.

*Red Dirt: Growing Up Okie,* Roxanne Dunbar-Ortiz (Verso, 1997). She describes her poor and working class Scots Irish family story as representative of the social construction of whiteness.

*White Lies: Race and the Myths of Whiteness,* Maurice Berger (Farrar, Strauss, and Giroux, 1999). Berger, who grew up poor and Jewish in Manhattan provides many vignettes illustrative of white privilege as he documents his struggles to understand how he "became" white.

### Movies on Video

The movies on this list are by and/or about people of color or about whites dealing with racism and white privilege. They are not documentaries or serious studies, but entertaining stories. Some were mainstream movies, while others had a more limited distribution. We suggest that you copy the list and carry it with you. Whenever you go to a video store, rent videos from the list.

Some of these movies replace narrow cultural stereotypes with representations from the broad spectrum of lives of people of color. Others present the stereotypes within a context that invites reflection and dialog. You will find white people attempting to understand and confront racism and white people acting out their privilege cluelessly. Many videos foreground the often messy dynamics of interracial interactions. Watch with a friend so you can talk about your reactions after.

| | |
|---|---|
| Amistad | American History X |
| American Me | The Associate |
| Bamboozled | Beat Street |
| Black and White | Bread and Roses |
| Brother From Another Planet | The Brothers |
| Bullworth | Center Stage |
| Chutney Popcorn | Clear Cut |
| Color Adjustment | Crooklyn |
| The Color Purple | Coming Home |
| Daughters of the Dust | Do the Right Thing |
| Double Happiness | Down to Earth |
| Down in the Delta | Eddie |
| Education of Little Tree | El Norte |
| Follow Me Home | Free of Eden |
| Friends | Grand Canyon |
| Get on the Bus | Girl Fight |
| Grand Avenue | Guess Who's Coming to Dinner |

| | |
|---|---|
| Hav Plenty | Hairspray |
| Higher Learning | Hoop Dreams |
| Incident at Oglala | Joy Luck Club |
| Jungle Fever | La Vida Loca |
| Life in a Bowl of Tea | Living Large |
| The Loretta Claiburn Story | Lotto Land |
| Love and Basketball | Love Songs |
| Luminarias | Mi Familia |
| Milagro Beanfield War | Mississippi Masala |
| Not In Our Town | Philadelphia |
| Pushing Hands | Remember the Titans |
| Rosewood | Save the Last Dance |
| School Daze | Selena |
| Set It Off | Six Degrees of Separation |
| Slam | Smoke Signals |
| Soul Food | Stand and Deliver |
| Tongues Untied | Tortilla Soup |
| What's Cooking | The Wedding Banquet |
| The Long Walk Home | Waiting to Exhale |
| Watermelon Woman | Zoot Suit |

## Training Videos

The following videos are available for purchase or rental and are used in diversity workshops and trainings. They are recommended here for both individual and group viewing followed by discussion.

### *Color of Fear*

A ground breaking film about the state of race relations in America as seen through the eyes of eight men of various ethnicities. Working from a psycho-social viewpoint, *Color of Fear* examines the effects that racism has had on each of the men. One by one, the men reveal the pain and scars that racism has caused them; the defense mechanism they use to survive, their fears of each other, and their hopes and visions for a multicultural society. [90 minutes]

Producer/Director: Lee Mun Wah
Stir-Fry Productions
1222 Preservation Park Way
Oakland, CA 94612
510-419-3930    510-419-3934 (fax)

### *The Eye of the Storm*

This documentary explores the nature of prejudice in a dramatic third-grade classroom experiment conducted in a small Midwestern town, a town without ghettos, blacks, or campus unrest. It demonstrates how quickly wholesome, friendly schoolchildren can be infected with the ugly virus of discrimination that leads to frustration, broken friendships, and vicious behavior. This is the story about the now famous Blue Eyes/Brown Eyes Experience conducted by Jane Elliot [25 minutes]

Distributor: The Center for Humanities
PO Box 1000
Mount Kisco, NY 10549-0010

### *Skin Deep*

A compelling tale of the complexities of race relations in America today, as experienced by a diverse group of college students. Through interviews, scenes from home and campus life, and in a chronicle of interracial dialogue at a weekend retreat, the program reveals deeply held attitudes and feelings, and outlines the challenges that remain in the quest for racial harmony. [57 minutes]

Producer/Director: Frances Reid
Iris Films, 1995
Call 1-800-343-5540 to order

### The Way Home

*The Way Home* shows what happened when eight ethnic councils of women came together to talk honestly about race, gender, and class in the U.S. The result is an unpredictable collection of stories that reveal the far-reaching effects of social oppression and present an inspiring picture of women moving beyond the duality of black and white. [92 minutes]

Producer/Director: Shakti Butler
World Trust
5920 San Pablo Ave
Oakland, CA 94608
877-WAYHOME    510-595-3281 (fax)
email: info@worldtrust.com
www.worldtrust.com

### Sankofa

Sankofa, an Akan word meaning "one must return to the past in order to move forward," is the story of the transformation of Mona, a self-possessed African American woman sent on a spiritual journey in time to experience the pain of slavery and the discovery of her African identity. (100 min.)

Mypheduh Films, Inc.
POB 10035
Washington, DC 20018-0035
202-289-6677 or 202-289-4477 (fax)
800-524-3895
Sankofa@cais.com

## Copyrights and Permissions

## About the Authors

Laurie B. Lippin, Ph.D., is the founder and CEO of Lippin & Associates, a consulting firm specializing in team building and diversity training to corporations, educational institutions, and nonprofit agencies. Dr. Lippin teaches at the University of California at Davis and is a certified senior MBTI (Myers-Briggs Type Indicator) training faculty member of the International Association of Psychological Type.

Judy Helfand is a community activist, writer, teacher, and Director of IMPACT Training. She is also a scholar focused on understanding the relationship between dominant culture in the U.S. and white identity and is committed to finding ways to help white people see our own whiteness.

Both believe strongly that those of us of European descent need to find ways to build antiracist actions into daily life and to find community with people of color.

For more information on Lippin & Associates and IMPACT Training, see: www.lippinassociates.com

The authors are available for training workshops or speaking engagements. Contact:

> Lippin & Associates at 707-792-1764 or
> Judy Helfand at judy@lippinassociates.com or 707-833-1890